I0459617

# THE
# FREEDOM
## TO
# *Feel*

## FINDING GOD IN THE MIDST
## OF GRIEF AND TRAUMA

# LEA TURNER RN, BSN

©2024 by Lea Turner

Published by hope*books
2217 Matthews Township Pkwy
Suite D302
Matthews, NC 28105
www.hopebooks.com

hope*books is a division of hope*media

Printed in the United States of America

All rights reserved. Without limiting the rights under copyrights reserved above, no part of this publication may be scanned, uploaded, reproduced, distributed, or transmitted in any form or by any means whatsoever without express prior written permission from both the author and publisher of this book—except in the case of brief quotations embodied in critical articles and reviews.

Thank you for supporting the author's rights.

First paperback edition.
Paperback ISBN: 979-8-89185-045-3
Hardcover ISBN: 979-8-89185-046-0
Ebook ISBN: 979-8-89185-047-7
Library of Congress Number: 2024931108

All Bible references are English Standard Version® (ESV®) Copyright © 2001 by Crossway, a publishing ministry of Good News Publishers unless otherwise noted. Other scripture references include:
The Message, (MSG), copyright © 1993, 2002, 2018 by Eugene H. Peterson.
The Holy Bible, New International Version®, NIV®. Copyright © 1973, 1978, 1984, 2011 by Biblica, Inc.™
*Holy Bible*, New Living Translation, (NLT), copyright ©1996, 2004, 2015 by Tyndale House Foundation. Used by permission of Tyndale House Publishers, Carol Stream, Illinois 60188.
The Living Bible, (TLB), copyright © 1971 by Tyndale House Foundation.
Holy Bible, Amplified, (AMP), Copyright © 2015 by The Lockman Foundation, La Habra, CA 90631.
And the King James Version (KJV). All rights reserved.

hope*books
hopebooks.com

# PRAISE FOR
# *THE FREEDOM TO FEEL*

Permission. On every page, Lea Turner offers it. Permission to grieve. Permission to feel. Permission to live.

She speaks to loss in a knowing way and approaches the many faces of grief as it sidles up to each of us time and time again. Lea is careful to remind us that there is no single path through pain. Rather, she takes us by the hand and whispers permission to us to feel—and heal.

—Ronne Rock, mentor, teacher, and author of
*One Woman Can Change the World*

Can the Lord be trusted in our hardship and suffering? Where is God in our grief? These are questions Lea Turner gives you permission to ask. Whether your heart hurts because of a wayward child, a medical diagnosis, or the wounds of living life with fallen people, Lea gives you space to process your doubts and fears without judgment and then points you right back to Christ. I'll recommend *The Freedom to Feel* to anyone walking a road she would never have chosen for herself. For in it, we see where the gospel meets us in our grief.

—Jill E. McCormick, writer, speaker, and host of the
*Grace In Real Life* podcast

As believers, many of us struggle with doubt, questioning our faith in life's darkest moments. *The Freedom to Feel* beautifully captures the essence of growth in the valley, where our relationship with God is often tested and transformed.

Lea's story dispels the myth that God is only present in times of joy and prosperity, bravely sharing her experiences of loss due to illness, fire, and addiction. My heart ached as I read the pages, and I found myself wondering again and again how she endured so much loss in such a short time.

The true beauty of this book is her unfiltered honesty about pain and loss. Grief often leads us to a place of isolation. Lea challenges us to embrace the freedom to feel and confront our wounds head-on, assuring us that we are not alone in our struggles. She encourages readers to dispel the misconception that God abandons us in suffering, offering a humble perspective on finding His goodness even in heartache.

For anyone seeking a transformative exploration of faith, grace, and resilience in the face of grief, *Freedom to Feel* is a compassionate guide and a testament to the enduring power of God's love and the healing that can emerge from despair.

—Kim Mosiman, author of *Reflections of Joy*

In *The Freedom to Feel*, Lea Turner invites us into her story and the Bible narrative to help us navigate our own grief journeys. She gives us permission to embrace our emotions and offers a hand-up with her comforting words.

—Dorina Lazo Gilmore-Young, Award-winning author of *Breathing Through Grief* and founder of Widow Mama Collective

*The Freedom to Feel* is a gift to the world. Lea's words and story are a balm conveying her experience and the heart of God. God writes a beautiful story of redemption and truly beauty comes from ashes. He's still writing.

–Pastor Cj Andrews, coach, speaker, and founder of Sacred Treasures

How do we manage hard emotions when the tidy life we wanted unravels in multiple losses? Lea's reflections through her grief from a father's death, a devastating house fire, a mother's diagnosis, and a child's addiction show us the breadth of heavy emotions while pointing to wholeness in Christ. *The Freedom to Feel* tackles the questions that come in ambiguous loss and cumulative grief and attests that even in pain, God breathes fresh hope.

–Lisa Appelo, author *Life Can Be Good Again: Putting Your World Back Together After It All Falls Apart*

*The Freedom to Feel* helps readers take steps to understanding how to maneuver through loss and unexpected suffering that bring deep grief. Lea invites readers to seek and trust God through the myriad of messy emotions grief brings. Using vivid images and personal experiences, the author skillfully weaves her own vulnerable account of grief with beautiful stories from the Bible, bringing readers rich insights into how to move through a healing journey. If you are facing grief and want to learn how to trust and uncover hope and joy again, this is the book for you!"

–Fern Buszowski, MA Counseling, MALM.
Author of *Embrace Life, Embrace Hope:*
*Cultivating Wholeness and Resilience through the Unexpected*

*To my husband and our five children
with whom I've walked this sacred ground.*

# TABLE OF CONTENTS

Praise For The Freedom to Feel................................................................iii

Foreword .............................................................................................ix

Introduction .......................................................................................xi

PART 1:  Embracing the Permission to Feel...............................1

CHAPTER 1: The Day My Life Changed .....................................3

CHAPTER 2: The Invitation ...........................................................17

CHAPTER 3: It's Okay to Feel.........................................................31

CHAPTER 4: Open Heart Surgery ...............................................41

CHAPTER 5: The Reality .................................................................55

CHAPTER 6: Where are You, God? ...............................................69

PART 2:  Discovering a New Mindset about Grief and Suffering.........81

CHAPTER 7: Looking and Seeing the Beauty for Ashes...........83

CHAPTER 8: It's Okay to Wrestle..................................................95

CHAPTER 9: Unmasking Shame...................................................107

CHAPTER 10: Unburdened by Forgiveness................................123

CHAPTER 11: Embracing the Release .........................................137

PART 3:  Cultivating a Soul Response ....................................153

CHAPTER 12: Unlikely Hope in Despair...................................155

CHAPTER 13: Limping with Grief and Dancing with Joy.....169

CHAPTER 14: Embracing the Physical Side of Grief and Trauma ........183

CHAPTER 15: The Healing Power of Community.....................193

THANKS .............................................................................................205

# FOREWORD

For over three decades, I have had the honor of shepherding communities and offering guidance and consolation as a pastor. Assisting others as they navigate the challenging terrain of grief and loss is no easy task. Within the pages of *The Freedom to Feel: Finding God in Grief and Trauma*, Lea Turner has encapsulated a truth, a kind of solace and understanding that I believe will bring real healing to those in pain. This book is more than Lea's recounting of personal trials—it is a beacon for all who have felt the cold touch of loss, the sting of betrayal, and the loneliness of despair. As you turn each page, I hope that you may find comfort in shared struggles, strength in vulnerability, and the courage to embrace every facet of your emotional being. Here lies not just a story but a journey—a pilgrimage of the heart towards the unfathomable peace that comes from truly feeling and, in feeling, finding the very heart of God.

Lea reminds us that life sometimes unfolds in such unexpected and devastating ways that the narrative of our existence is forever altered. The words within these pages are a testament to such a transformation— where the cruel twists of fate force a reckoning with our deepest beliefs about control, security, and faith.

As I journeyed through these writings, I realized this book goes beyond grief and loss; it challenges the core of our faith and our efforts to steer through life's unpredictable currents. It acknowledges that despite meticulous planning and preparation, life can shift suddenly, compelling us to seek comfort and strength in the most unforeseen places.

As you make your way through this book, you may discover that your understanding of suffering and providence is challenged. You may be compelled to reexamine the notion that we can control life with the right planning and enough faith. Through raw and honest reflections, Lea invites us to witness her struggle and possibly see our lives reflected in the turmoil and the eventual finding of hope amidst the ruins.

Chapter after chapter, the resilience of the human spirit shines forth, as does the profound truth that sometimes, in the most broken places, we discover the true depth of our faith and the comforting presence of a God who is with us, even in the ashes.

Welcome to a brave space where healing begins with the simplest yet most profound permission: the freedom to feel.

Jody Andrews, *Co-Founder of Sacred Life Inc., Pastor of Life Church in Columbus, Mississippi*

# INTRODUCTION

In the darkest corners of our lives where pain and suffering reside, we find ourselves stripped of the freedom to feel, blindsided by the moment, unraveling the threads of our seemingly ordinary life, plunging us into a wilderness of pain and uncertainty. The weight of hell is pressing up against our chests, and we want to scream, but we can't. In these moments of pain, we become entangled in a web of emotions, suffocating under the weight of sadness, shock, and disbelief. There's no tidy pattern to the pain and suffering we feel. We're crushed under the weight of it and have no idea what to do. I know this place intimately, for it is where my story unfolds.

I'd walked through life's ups and downs with others, witnessing their struggles and offering support, but I'd never genuinely experienced the unbearable weight of grief until this fateful day.

The day starts like any other. One minute, I feel carefree; the next, my world shatters into a million pieces. It's still hard to believe.

I sat in a bustling nail salon several years ago, enjoying a girls' weekend. Laughter and the rhythm of pampering fill the air. Little did I know my world was about to be turned upside down.

My phone rings, and I instantly feel a sense of dread. It's the call we all fear, the one bringing unexpected news capable of shaking the foundations of our existence.

"Your dad fell, and we're sitting in the emergency room waiting for results," my mom's voice crackles on the other end. Time seems to freeze. Profound sadness, shock, and disbelief wash over me like a tidal wave, threatening to engulf my fragile state of being.

Up until this point, my parents were healthy and stable. Sure, my dad struggled with sinus infections, but nothing a little antibiotic couldn't fix.

I hang up the phone after telling my mom I'll pray because that's all you can do when life is uncontrollable.

Sitting surrounded by the familiar scent of nail polish and the buzz of conversations, I wrestle with a whirlwind of emotions. My mind begins playing an endless negative script of all that might go wrong. Attempting to grasp onto faith, desperately trying to find peace in the chaos, I whisper to myself, "Oh, it's nothing. He'll be fine," trying to mask my gnawing fear, having no idea that this is only the beginning of my journey through the unfathomable depths of grief and trauma.

A few hours pass and a second phone call comes from my mom as we drive home. She says it slowly, and her voice cracks as the words spill out: "They found a brain tumor, and your father will be undergoing surgery next week."

My whole life—stops.

In one second, my world comes to a halt. My body is still, so still, it might have given out under me. The weight of her words sink deep into my being, and a sense of profound loss washes over me.

Fighting back tears as I hang up the phone, memories and emotions rush through my mind. I think back to all the moments I shared with my father—the laughter, the guidance, the warmth of his presence. How can this be happening? What will I do without my father? He is too young to face such a dire threat. A cocktail of emotions swirls within—fear, anger, helplessness, and a gnawing sense of grief.

I ask my friend to drive the rest of the way home because an hour's drive is a long time to hold it together. As soon as I feel the hard passenger seat, I curl up into a ball and crumble into a million pieces as the tears flow. The moment's heaviness fills the car as if even the atmosphere mourns alongside me. I need the script running in my head to say everything will be okay, but nothing about this seems okay.

The following eight months are hell—a complete nightmare. Eight long months of flying back and forth to my parents' home in North Carolina, caught in a relentless cycle of hope and despair, of doctor visits and hospital stay after hospital stay, each day bringing new tests, treatments, and more waves of uncertainty.

Cancer destroys my father's body and causes his once vibrant spirit to wane under the weight of his illness. The toll it takes on his body and mind is evident, his once-strong frame reduced to a mere shadow of its former self. But even among the pain and suffering, there were moments of peace— in the presence of family, gathering around him like a shield of love and cherishing moments of laughter, soaking in every moment.

Desperate to grant his dying wish, we medically transported him to Mississippi, where his beloved grandchildren surrounded him with love.

The eighth-month period seemed like an eternity, yet also a blink of an eye. And then suddenly, during our collective prayers and fervent longing for a miracle, he is gone. The loss cut through us like a jagged blade, leaving behind an indelible void. It is a devastating blow, shattering our dreams and leaving us in a sea of grief.

In the coming years, I received five devastating phone calls, each ushering in a new and unique wave of pain and suffering, rearranging my entire being. Yet, through it, God reveals things in myself and my belief system that caused me to question everything—my faith, identity, and even the very character of God. I stumble through the wilderness of darkness, desperately seeking a way out. I wonder if grief will ever truly leave. And if it does, who will I be? Will my faith survive? Why in the world did God allow all this suffering into my life? Question after question—and with tears rolling down my face, two words slip out, "Why me?"

In the wake of devastation, I grapple with a mixture of despair and a faint glimmer of hope intermingling in a fragile dance within my heart. I am lost in a whirlwind of emotions, unsure of how to navigate the treachery of grief and uncertainty. The journey ahead seems daunting, filled with winding paths threatening to engulf me in their darkness.

But amidst the darkness, there are flickers of unexpected peace, moments where I sense the presence of God even in my despair. Through it all, I discovered grief is not a problem to be solved or dismissed but rather an invitation to experience more of God's love and grace. In my brokenness, I begin to see His goodness shining through.

As a believer, you can't go through times like this without questioning your faith, wondering what God is up to, and doubting His goodness and faithfulness. But this is where the growth happens: in the valley. Many facets of peace and unexpected awakenings to God's presence show up in the darkness, redefining our walk with Him. The pain is real, but so is His goodness—and there is a path out of the darkness.

*And I'm not alone.*

None of us live a pain-free life. All of us are wounded by disappointments and losses, and at some point, they may break us. Even though grief is universal, it can feel like a wilderness of pain and emotions that we're navigating alone.

The reality is we are never alone, but it takes breaking ties with the lie that God is good only when life is good to rest in this truth. Believing no one is there for us only causes us to minimize our pain and move on. The truth is God's not ghosting us, causing us to rock our bodies in grief and suffering alone.

As I write, I wonder what unexpected moments you've encountered. Did they come in the form of a phone call with a diagnosis? Or did the news come of a sudden death or tragedy? Perhaps your unexpected moment isn't a phone call. Maybe it's a teenager staggering in drunk or giving the news of a pregnancy. Or maybe it's a husband admitting an affair. Our unexpected moments may look different, but we all feel unprepared and struggle to navigate these feelings in the wilderness of darkness.

The hard truth is: There's no white-knuckling ourselves out of grief and sorrow.

Cultural values of strength and resilience teach us to hide our emotions. Messages urging us to put on a brave face, keep a stiff upper lip, and move on are everywhere. But in this relentless pursuit of acceptance, we lose something precious—the freedom to feel.

Our society constructs an intricate façade, shunning vulnerability and deeming it a sign of weakness. Conditioned to believe that displaying emotions is an act of self-indulgence or attention-seeking, we hide our tears, grief, and heartache behind a mask of stoic composure. In doing so, we deny ourselves the essence of our humanity—the raw, unfiltered experience of the full spectrum of emotions.

It rarely occurs to us that suppressing our emotions can cause us to become estranged from God and one another. When we white-knuckle through grief, we forfeit a deeper bond with God in the depths of our feelings. It's hard to believe, but when we fully experience our emotions, we create space for God to meet us in our vulnerability. In our tears, He offers His comforting embrace. In our anger, He provides His gentle guidance, and in our despair, He shows His unwavering hope. In the rawness of our emotions, we encounter a God who is not distant or aloof but intimately involved in every aspect of our lives.

Pastor John Ortberg unravels this truth in his book *Soul Keeping*.[1] "If you ask people who don't believe in God why they don't, the number one reason will be suffering. If you ask people who believe in God when they grew most spiritually, the number one answer will be suffering."

Our emotions can become a conduit for spiritual growth as we surrender our burdens to God and allow His presence to infuse our healing journey. In the freedom to feel, we open ourselves to divine encounters where God's love meets us in the depths of our sorrow and transforms our brokenness into beauty.

We can't be afraid of grief and suffering. Our grief matters to God. If we can confront our pain, we'll experience a greater awareness of God and His promises through our suffering…

Now more than ever, it is imperative to challenge this cultural narrative. We must reclaim the freedom to feel, for it is within the depths of our emotions that we will find healing, growth, and profound connection. Honoring our pain and allowing ourselves to experience the depths of our sorrow opens the door to true authenticity and genuine connection with ourselves and others.

The path to healing lies not in denying our pain but in the freedom to feel it all—the raw, unfiltered emotions that surge within us. In the depths of our sorrow, we encounter a God who meets us in our pain, embraces our vulnerability, and guides us through the maze of grief

---

[1] John Ortberg, *Soul Keeping: Caring for the Most Important Part of You* (United States: Zondervan, 2014), 179.

toward a place of peace and joy found only in Him.

In the pages of *The Freedom to Feel*, I invite you to join me on a transformative journey through the wilderness of grief and suffering, where we'll navigate the depths of pain and embrace the freedom to feel. Together, we'll confront our deepest wounds, explore the questions plaguing our hearts, and discover a path forward. Even in our darkest moments, we can emerge with a renewed sense of hope and find peace and joy in the arms of a loving God.

It's an invitation to break free from societal expectations and the pressure to mask our pain. Within these pages, we'll learn how to navigate the complexities of grief, find peace in God's presence, and ultimately reclaim our freedom to feel.

We will delve into the rich tapestry of spiritual practices, prayer, and contemplation, seeking to deepen our intimacy with God as we navigate the complexities of grief and trauma. As I share my story through reflections on faith, resilience, reflective exercises, and scriptural insights, we will cultivate a path that will lead us to experience God's presence more profoundly and authentically, emerging on the other side with renewed purpose and a deeper connection to Him. It's not a journey for the faint of heart but for those willing to embark on a life-changing voyage towards freedom, healing, and a deeper understanding of who we are in God.

Don't think of this as a guide on how to grieve. It's simply words from a friend who's been through her share of pain, offering comfort and encouragement. I certainly don't write because I have it all figured out or because I have a secret formula on how living through suffering creates a fairy-tale life. I write because I've discovered the hope we long for isn't in the pain-free life; it's in the messy and gut-wrenching grief. We no longer need to despise the pain but see it as a highway to an encounter with God.

I pen these words not as a scholar or grief expert. I am neither a pastor nor a theologian. I am a fellow wilderness wanderer hoping to give words to your pain, to hold space for you to feel, and to encourage you to see God's goodness.

May this book serve as a guiding light in the darkness, offering hope and comfort to those navigating their journeys of grief and trauma. May it remind us our pain is not in vain but open us up to the transformative power of God's love in embracing the freedom to feel. Remember, you're not alone in your grief, my friend. Together, we'll uncover the beauty in holding space for our suffering and discover the profound healing that comes when we give ourselves *The Freedom to Feel.*

# PART 1

## EMBRACING
## THE PERMISSION TO FEEL

# CHAPTER 1

## THE DAY MY LIFE CHANGED

> *O GOD, look at the trouble I am in!*
> *My stomach in knots, my heart wrecked...*
> *—Lamentations 1:20, MSG*

It's still hard to believe that July 30, 2020, will always be remembered as the day that changed my life.

It's a two-hour drive home from my mom's oncology appointment. The first hour goes by quickly as my mom and I discuss her prognosis and how my fourteen-year-old daughter, Abby, manages the house and her three younger siblings well while I'm out of town. Even though she's the second oldest, she functions much like the oldest child since her older brother works a lot.

I look over at my mom, thinking that barely four months have slipped by since receiving the jarring second unexpected call on Easter. Her voice echoes my disbelief as she says, "I think something's wrong." I remember sitting in the nearest chair, listening as she explained her symptoms. I keep tracing the day's events, attempting to understand it all. How could a call like this come on the day we celebrate Jesus' resurrection?

Only hours before, we sit watching church online because we are confined to our houses to stop the spread of a crazy virus. Resurrection biscuits are made, and the kids laugh and hunt for eggs in the backyard. Throughout the day, Mom and I spend hours at the stove, preparing a meal to commemorate the finished work of the Cross. As we gather around the table, everything feels oddly normal. However, this Easter marks the first holiday since my dad's passing. Unbeknownst to us, more distressing news awaits.

Shortly after she leaves my house, my mom calls to report that she is bleeding. I know what these symptoms will mean. A few days of testing confirmed cancer—a word I didn't want to hear so soon. Suddenly, I fear the future as never before.

Please, not my mom. She's the only parent I have left. What will I do without her? How do you wander through life without a parent to love and support you? What in the world lies ahead? And how is God glorified through this?

Selfishly, I wrestle with not wanting to sit in hospital rooms and stale doctor's offices only eight months after caring for my dad. Slapping that nasty, ugly word cancer on my only living parent makes me want to scream and run and say "not-nice" words because it's all so unfair. I know the unwanted waves of grief will keep crashing over and over like tsunami waves, seemingly out of nowhere, for a long time.

As we continue driving home from her post-op appointment, we discuss my mom's upcoming chemotherapy. Unaware life is about to take another sharp turn. In a fragile attempt to normalize life with suffering, I remember thinking: I hope there will be enough time to enjoy the rest of the day with the kids once we get home.

I long to make the most of the time left in the summer because you can't control how the river winds and bends. Sometimes, there are rapids, and sometimes it's smooth sailing. It's the same with life. You can't control the river, but you can manage your response to the bends in the journey. However, being present and enjoying each moment isn't easy when your mind is preoccupied with doctor's appointments and the constant ache of wondering if life will ever return to normal.

Our family may roast marshmallows in the last few weeks of summer or take another trip to the local pool. Or possibly go back to school shopping. Since COVID abruptly ended last school year, excitement for the upcoming school year has been building. Our oldest is beginning his senior year, and the youngest is starting preschool.

Our life is full, bursting with chaotic energy. Being a wife and raising five kids ranging from teens to school-aged requires full attention, which leaves few emotional resources available to me during this season. Amidst the hustle and bustle, I often get caught up in the whirlwind of daily tasks, always striving to check off the never-ending to-do list. The preparations seem endless when school starts, especially with five children.

At 11:20 am, a text arrives, accompanied by a photo of our living room—pristine and tidy, a testament to my daughter Abby's dedication. She spends the morning cleaning and organizing, taking pride in helping me maintain our home. After moving just seven months ago, we finally feel settled. The house is buzzing with activity as friends come and go, savoring the last precious days of summer. Earlier in the day, Brandon, my eleven-year-old, had friends over—a simple joy we took for granted before the months of COVID-induced quarantine.

Little do we know that danger silently lurkers amidst the laughter and joy in our home. It isn't until Abby settles on the living room couch that she notices the smoke. Time stands still as she realizes the raging flames had been devouring our attic for nearly an hour. Panic washes over her, and she immediately calls for her two brothers and runs to grab her three-year-old sister from her nap.

They all get out of the house just in time.

An hour after receiving the first text, my phone rings with Abby frantically uttering the fearful and desperate words no parent ever wants to hear: "Mom, our house is on fire."

Wait. What?

"Who left the oven on? What do you mean, 'fire'?" My mind can't focus.

What in the world is she talking about? She is making no sense.

"No, Mom, like the house… it's in flames. It's gone."

The world around me freezes as adrenaline courses through my veins. Fear and disbelief clutch my heart, threatening to suffocate me. In an instant, the safety and stability we have taken for granted crumbles before our eyes, consumed by an unforgiving inferno. The normalcy we fought so hard to regain after my father's death and my mom's cancer diagnosis shattered into a thousand pieces, leaving us adrift in a sea of uncertainty.

This third unexpected call brings with it what experts call trauma.

My world goes dark as I call my neighbor to be with the children. Confusion clouds my mind, and my thoughts are rambling. What could be happening to us? How did I get from talking to my mom to this horrid nightmare? My brain can't make sense of it all. Looking back, I can see that I am going numb.

Unbeknownst to me, my children stand barefoot and alone, screaming for our dog caught in the house, who never emerges. We never do find her body. Terrified, they wait for my neighbor to arrive for what feels like an eternity.

Unfortunately, you can't always protect your children from the nightmare of real life.

We lose everything.

Later, we discovered flames were billowing from the attic minutes before my daughter's call, and an hour before that, she heard crackling noises upstairs. Except, there is no upstairs, just an attic. It's a miracle that Abby grabbed her sister and ensured her two brothers had gotten out. They barely escaped the house before it erupted into flames.

It's a grueling hour of helplessness before my mom and I arrive to help my children.

One hour of feeling vulnerable and small, calling out to God, repeatedly asking, How do I walk my family through something like this? Oh, God, why?

I see smoke rising above the trees as we drive into the neighborhood. I have no idea that desperately broken days are ahead. I am sure we'll figure out how to make it through together, except there's no handbook for handling something like this. I spend the next few years trying to mend my family back into one piece. During those "knocked-off-my-feet" years, grief from unexpected losses was almost too much to bear. I never imagined our life taking such a drastic turn for the worse.

Maybe it's good that we don't know how to live through the pain of a sudden catastrophe. Perhaps that's where our trust in God comes in. The human heart wants to ask, "But will it all be okay if I let go and trust God in the unknown?" Maybe this is where faith comes in, and our trust in God has a chance to grow.

When tragedy strikes, who *isn't* desperately fumbling around in the dark, trying to formulate a plan, and looking for the silver lining? Who doesn't want a guarantee that everything will turn out okay? We recite to ourselves, *"For I know the plans I have for you,' declares the Lord, 'plans for a hope and a future"* (Jeremiah 29:11). Plans for me? For good? For *hope*?

What if God has a different kind of good in mind than we do?

I just want to wake up from this nightmare with no trauma from the straight-out-of-nowhere tragedy of a house fire. Without continuous depression, feelings of abandonment, or excessive anxiety, and without endless nights questioning whether life will ever return to normalcy, no struggling teenagers in the aftermath, leaving me clueless about how to support them.

There are so many layers to our family's story. Over the years, I've often wondered if we'll ever heal from all of this. Will we ever be the same again?

Why do we foolishly think life will never have unexpected curves on the road? Did I actually believe God would never allow something hard into my life? Expecting life always to go as planned doesn't ultimately make any sense.

And yet, that's what our society and culture preaches.

There aren't funerals for this kind of thing. We didn't lose a child to the fire, but we did lose our pet and our home. Yes, we are thankful God spared our lives, yet life as we knew it was over. Life was going as planned one minute, and the next, it wasn't. We are experiencing the death of our life as we knew it.

Trauma rearranges our entire lives. Although I try to dismiss the pain and count my blessings, the unbearable pain remains. Many people around us struggle to understand the pain of losing twenty years of belongings and memories to a fire. They can't fully grasp the trauma from the house fire and the deep wounds that it leaves.

But God can turn this into good, right? But what if He doesn't do what we pray for, then what?

One of the reasons suffering scares us is that it forces us to surrender control over our lives. Suffering rearranges the plans we've mapped out for our lives. Welcome to a life where Plan A turns into Plan Z. When we can't follow a ten-year plan, we're forced to face our lack of control.

When we lose control, we attempt to regain it as quickly as possible, as if nothing happened. The thing is, we never had control in the first place. I once saw an old bumper sticker that said, "Jesus is my copilot." Here's the thing: Jesus isn't our copilot. He's the pilot. So, no matter what we do, we have no control over our lives.

Does the fact that none of us are in control of this life ruffle your theology a bit? Is there a *but, but, but…* welling up inside you, trying to explain how our prayers can shape our future, and if we follow a well-mapped-out plan, we will get satisfactory results?

Paul Tripp writes, "Suffering has the power to expose what you've been trusting all along."[2]

Amid the pain, we sit among the ashes, silently grieving our shattered dreams while echoes of sermons promising a life without suffering reverberate. By embracing the illusion of a flawlessly orchestrated life with no suffering, we're essentially worshiping a false God we created in our minds. This misguided theology leads us to feel deserted by God in our trials, fostering a sense of hopelessness as we blame ourselves for the pain we endure.

In an attempt to regain control of our lives, we minimize our pain

---

[2] Paul David Tripp, *Suffering* (Chicago: Crossway, 2018), 21.

and trauma by comparing stories, grasping to find the silver lining to escape our reality. Yet, realizing we've lost control is the beginning of the grief journey. All pain and suffering are worthy of being brought into the light.

So, I'm here to tell you that your wounds and trauma *matter*, and you've done nothing to deserve this pain. Life is hard and painful in a million different ways. You are not alone in your suffering. Even if you're wounded, there's no need to put up walls of shame and guilt. There's nothing you can do to prevent further suffering. Grief is a psycho-spiritual process, not just related to death. Grief can come from the loss of anything. You can't compare your grief with someone else's, just like you can't minimize anyone's trauma or loss. It's all painful, and it all needs to be acknowledged.

Ignoring the pain, shrinking it, or pretending it isn't hard because someone else's suffering seems worse isn't heroic. Instead, it dismisses the love and nearness God is trying to reveal to you in the darkness you face.

As we approach the burning house, I tell my mom to drive straight to the neighbor's house, where the children are taking refuge. I can't muster the strength to witness our home engulfed in flames, and truth be told, I never did.

Sometimes, it takes time to face reality and devastation head-on. So, instead, I do my best to comfort the children, their tears mingling with mine. For the first time, I fully understand that my life is beyond my control. I can't protect my kids from the road ahead and wipe away the anguish on their innocent faces or mine. Trauma and loss force us to confront the stark truth that life's course is not within our grasp.

I lie in the darkness that night, my entire body feeling the day's weight. Mike, my husband, snores while Abby sleeps on the floor beside us. We are in a one-room mother-in-law suite a friend graciously allowed us to stay in. All I can remember is how darkness surrounded me and how alone I felt.

What exactly is happening? And for an instant, I wonder, Where are you, God?

I imagined my life going differently.

Two people at the beginning of time probably thought the same thing.

I bet Adam and Eve never dreamed of life taking such a drastic turn. One minute, they're enjoying intimacy with God and each other, and the next, they're walking out of Eden with shattered dreams. Completely broken.

A howling, shrieking, screaming mass of pain engulfed their beings because they had grasped for control they were never meant to obtain.

*"Did God actually say?"* the serpent asked Eve. Failure to bring this very question to God broke intimacy with her Father.

They felt the raw reality of grief that day, and so did God.

In a moment of weakness, Eve's questioning of the words of her Creator caused division. Running and hiding, Adam and Eve grabbed leaves to cover the pain of what once was. *Had God abandoned them?*

I imagine a wave of sadness engulfing Eve's heart and, for the first time, the first feeling of grief. She mourned a life that didn't turn out the way she thought, grieving for all that she lost. Each dream she held for her children intensified this sorrow, crashing over her like relentless waves. Life unexpectedly took a turn for the worse, and suddenly, she wondered where God was, and I wonder if she blamed herself – just like us.

We can't let the lies of the darkness become the truth in the light.

> *But the Lord God called to the man and said to him,*
> *"Where are you?"* (Genesis 3:9)

When we ask where God is, He's already calling us. God hasn't left. He's not hiding from us. It pains God to see us fumble in the darkness, questioning whether He's there. God reaches out to us because he longs to connect with our hearts. God doesn't keep us from suffering; He wants us to experience his love piercing through it. He is forever and always pulling us closer and whispering, *Where are you?*

God's intentions with these three words were also to jolt Adam and Eve into the reality of their situation and begin to take inventory of their emotions and feelings. Had they processed what just happened? Being brutally honest penetrates the darkness with light, even if it's just a flicker. Keeping ourselves at a distance from grief cannot keep us from being consumed by it.

Right now, God is whispering to you and me: *Where are you?*

Before speaking anything into existence, God was there. At the very beginning of time, he was present. There was not one moment where he ghosted. *"Now the earth was formless and empty, darkness was over the surface of the deep, and the Spirit of God was hovering over the waters"* (Genesis 1:2).

The verb used for "hovering" shows up only in one other place in the Bible: Deuteronomy 32:11, where it describes a mother bird beating her wings over her little ones, encouraging them to fly.[3]

He's not conquering the darkness as the Spirit hovers because *He's already conquered it.* And He's not dismissing the darkness as if it doesn't exist or demanding meaning. He's not pretending it's light. He's loving and fostering it as a mother bird does with its young. God's spirit isn't part of the darkness. The Holy Spirit is motherly love, bringing comfort and life-sustaining nutrients to an otherwise formless void.

God hovered over the darkness at the beginning of time, bringing life, and He's hovering over our lives now, doing the same. Hope diminishes when we stop believing God hovers over our darkness. And *"by his light, I walked through darkness"* (Job 29:3). God never intended for suffering to separate us from His presence. The startling truth is suffering is the most incredible avenue for deeper intimacy. If only we could turn toward God, letting His love touch the painful parts of ourselves that we try to hide or bury.

---

[3] FR. George Montague, "He Still Hovers over Chaos," The Word Among Us, 2021, https://wau.org/resources/article/re_he_still_hovers_over_chaos/.

In the middle of David's crushing moments of grief, he utters, *"I will pour my hope in God! I will praise him again- my Savior and my God."*[4]

Several days before the fire, Mike and I sit under a blanket of stars, taking in the beauty of the summer night sky. We often come here to recap the day's events, plan the coming days, and reconnect as a married couple. With five kids and Mike's demanding job, we intentionally keep our twenty-year marriage romance alive. We don't know it then, but these moments hold us together through the fierce winds. So it is with God.

But since COVID-19, making time for each other isn't easy. For the first time, I am struggling with depression. Being a caregiver for my dad for seven months and then grieving his passing took a toll on me. Our oldest son also begins to leak his pain. His wrong choices start to steer him down a slippery slope of struggles involving pot, pills, alcohol, and troubled relationships—his bad decisions will eventually lead to my most tremendous loss and most painful grief.

There's no grave site to visit, just shattered dreams.

As my husband and I lie together, I see the stars in a new way. Bright and clear, not a cloud to cover them. Burning through the darkness, they light up the whole sky. In the following months, reflecting on this moment grounds me. Even if our world is chaotic, the stars remain the same, burning through the darkness.

And there it is again in His word, *"...that God is light and in Him is no darkness at all"* (John 1:8).

Even the dark is not truly dark.

There's comfort in knowing God is light. It means our world can't truly snuff out even in our darkest hour. God's grandeur and the righteousness of his pursuit for us do not change when our life goes dim. And there it is in Genesis, the light is day and the evening darkness, yet God speaks them into existence with one single phrase, *"Let there be light."*

We see this truth in Colossians 1:15-20:

---

[4] Psalm 42:11 NLT.

*"The Son is the image of the invisible God, the firstborn over all creation. For in him, all things were created: things in heaven and on earth, visible and invisible, whether thrones or powers or rulers or authorities; all things have been created through him and for him. He is before all things, and in him, all things hold together. And he is the head of the body, the church; he is the beginning and the firstborn from among the dead, so that in everything he might have the supremacy. For God was pleased to have all his fullness dwell in him, and through him to reconcile to himself all things, whether things on earth or things in heaven, by making peace through his blood, shed on the cross."*

Considering that Jesus, the Lord of all creation, binds the universe together, can we trust Him despite our suffering? Can we trust Jesus to be the satisfaction of our souls? Remembering these brightly shining stars each night guides me through the darkest nights, grounding me in God.

So it is with grief, unique as every single star. Grief is a fragile place to be and an exercise in futility. I'm learning the key is to permit yourself to weep when there are no words while looking forward with hope-felt eyes to the coming promise. Releasing the lie that tears are a sign of weakness and a lack of faith allows us to embrace sadness with faith because we anticipate the coming of our Savior.

The next day after the fire, Mike and I feel gathered and soothed by God's presence as we assess the remains of what was once our home. I don't brush away the tears streaming down my face, clouding my vision. I yield to the grief, and I feel something. Allowing myself to lament the reality of what was lost draws God into my pain.

I remember, *"The Lord is near to the brokenhearted and saves the crushed in spirit"* (Psalm 34:18). As my vision clears, I spot a sign hanging on my daughter's bedroom wall that reads:

"I am
The daughter of a king
Who is not moved by the
World for my God is with
Me and goes before me I do
Not fear because I am
His."

It's a miracle the sign remains. Only the stud that the sign hangs on remains. I'm in awe.

God's presence never left us, even when our house was burning. He held the flames back as our children ran out the door, escaping the explosion within minutes. He went before them in their time of need, just as he goes before us in ours.

I feel like Job, who lost everything. My dad died from a rare brain tumor. My mom is now walking through treatments for uterine cancer. And if that isn't enough, now my house has burned to the ground. So I have every right to turn my back on God—right? The instability of life gives way to raw and fragile emotions. Even though we feel alone, we're not, for Jesus himself is *"a man of sorrows, acquainted with the grief"* (Isaiah 53:3).

I don't question God's presence in the darkness. I feel God hovering. My mind struggles to accept the dark, desolate valley God's allowing my family to walk through. In a million different ways, I feel like I'm Mary standing outside the tomb of Jesus, hopeless about the future.

I underlined three verses in my Bible a few days after the fire: *"Now Mary stood outside the tomb crying. As she wept, she bent over to look into the tomb"* (John 20:11).

I wonder if a wave of grief overwhelmed Mary, leaving her breathless as she searched for Jesus in the cavernous tomb. This man who loved her died, and she felt the sting of loss. Grief clouded her vision, causing her to mistake Jesus for the gardener. It wasn't until Jesus spoke her name that she saw Him and clung to Him.

Just as God called Mary, He calls out our names during our grief. Mary cried for what was lost while allowing Jesus to infuse her with faith for future promises.

So this is it: Walking through the darkness isn't about making sense of it or finding meaning. It's about allowing our pain and suffering to guide us to the hope and promises of Jesus. It's about allowing ourselves to feel our reality while standing in faith for the future.

---

## DIGGING DEEPER:

1. Have you ever imagined a different trajectory for your life, only to face the stark reality that things turned out drastically different? Consider the story of Adam and Eve, who never anticipated the devastating turn of their lives. Reflect on the brokenness they experienced when they grasped for control they were never meant to obtain. How does their story resonate with your journey of unmet expectations and shattered dreams?

2. In moments of doubt and questioning, have you ever felt distant from God, as if He has abandoned you? Recall the story of Eve, whose questioning God's words led to a division in her intimacy with Him. Reflect on the moments when you have doubted God's presence and questioned His plans. How can you navigate the tension between grief, doubt, and the truth that God is always near, even amidst darkness? Consider the significance of God calling out to Adam, asking, "Where are you?" How does this invitation to honest dialogue with God offer hope and healing in your journey of grief and uncertainty?

# CHAPTER 2

## THE INVITATION

> *"Home is allowing Him to lead me into new and unexpected territory, trusting that although I may find it unfamiliar, He has already gone before. He knows the way, and He won't leave me lost and alone"* [5]

It feels like a million trillion trees are stretching over where we walk. Each tree looks the same, and I'm sure we passed the same one more than once. Our feet ache, and our bodies are beyond sore. As the night sky approaches, the path becomes less and less visible. The weight of our book bags and the weight crushing our spirits—the fear, the disbelief, the anger—all blur together as we continue walking and realize we are lost.

There seems to be no end in sight of our little hike in the woods.

If your sister-in-law, who also has a bundle of children, calls to invite you on a girl's weekend to the mountains of New York, you go without a second thought. Everything falls into place, and a few weeks later, I find myself boarding a plane for the first time since tragedy struck.

"Excited" is an understatement. We are anticipating a wonderful weekend with some much-needed R&R and many laughs.

"Want to go on a twelve-mile hike? Six miles up and six miles back?"

---

[5] Michele Cushatt, *I Am* (Grand Rapids: Zondervan, 2017), 77.

My sister-in-law asks me the first morning there.

I pause, mildly amused by this question, and answer, "Are you crazy?! We came here to rest and relax. Is there a shorter hike?"

We agree instead on a hike that will only take six miles total, allowing us time to rest and read a book. The brochure indicates a beautiful waterfall and an outlook with a fantastic view. As we begin walking, we know this shorter hike will be much easier.

Three hours later, with no waterfall in sight, we wondered if we were on the right trail. That sometimes happens when you're on a journey. You anticipate an outcome and time frame, but then you get lost. The flawlessly curated plan you mapped out for your life crumbles, and you begin to question if maybe, just maybe, you did something wrong along the way. What happened?

Looking different from the brochure, we think we have taken a wrong turn. Three hours in, and we haven't seen anything except trees. Where are we?

Where's the promised outlook and waterfall? And shouldn't we be there by now? Sound familiar? I feel my anxiety rising, realizing this is not what I expected to happen.

We're lost.

*Expectations can destroy our trust in others, especially God.*

As each mile rolled into the next, each step felt heavier and heavier. My sister-in-law finally admitted she may have made a mistake.

"What do you mean, 'a mistake'? I thought you looked at the map. I thought we had a plan," I responded.

It's not the difficulty of the journey that crushes us; it's that the journey isn't going as planned, and we have to adjust.

Somehow, my sister-in-law and I had parked the car and begun the three-mile hike from the wrong starting point. This mistake cost us time and days of aches and pains. But most of all, we thought it cost the promise of the waterfall and outlook. We considered turning around for a split second but had gone too far to turn back now. There was no other option but to continue onward.

We kept walking, unsure if we'd find our way back to the car. *Would we have to be airlifted back?* I learned it requires courage and bravery to continue rather than avoid mistakes or give up altogether.

*We had no option.*

The six-mile hike turned into a thirteen-mile hike! Because sometimes, the journey takes longer than expected, and airlifting out is not an option. To our surprise, we stumbled upon the waterfall and lookout, savoring them a little bit more because of the effort it took to get there. Sometimes, God invites us to walk *through* what looks like a wilderness to reach the promise.

You need to know I'm not a hiker; this was my first hike *ever*! If you had told me I'd be hiking thirteen miles, I would have thought you were crazy and returned to bed.

You may be thinking the same thing about your situation. If God had peeled back the future and you saw what you'd be walking *through* today, you'd panic.

Much like that hike, I wandered in a wilderness of grief for two solid years, lost and confused, questioning if I'd ever see God's fulfilled promises. I had no idea how to live while grieving, so I quoted verses on God's peace in an attempt to numb my rising feelings. Most days, I didn't know what to do with my emotions. *Would the ache and restlessness disappear one day?* Deep inside, where no one saw, including myself, was profound sadness.

Grief can feel like a wilderness.

Our surroundings blur, and we feel as if we're walking in circles. Darkness and joylessness enveloped us. Our entire body aches as if we've been run over by a bus. We often can't find the words to express the depth of our pain. It can feel lonely and bewildering. The life we had expected is now unreachable. Instead of the promised fairy tale, the journey is arduous, filled with suffering and pain. The temptation is to pretend nothing had happened while desperately seeking an escape from the suffering and pain. We oftentimes feel the need to blame God and others: *this can't possibly be the right trail.*

Loss can rearrange your entire world, and there seems to be no way to wade through all the emotions. You're navigating the uncharted and treacherous land of the unknowns of *"What's next?" "Why did this happen?" "How could this have been prevented?"* and *"Where is God?"* The questions go on and on, stealing sleep and rest. You question if you made a wrong turn somewhere and if you're doing this grieving thing right.

*You're in a wilderness.*

Years later, after the trip with my sister-in-law, I stand at the kitchen sink in need of more than Christian clichés and phrases like: "Everything is going to be okay." Here at the sink, with crumbs across the counter and pots stacked that need scrubbing, with tears rolling down my cheek, I prayed for the unbearable pain to stop—prayed for God to break the silence.

No matter how hard I tried or how much I longed for wholeness or a glimmer of hope, the pain remained. Unfortunately, my exhausted efforts of striving through my grief weren't working. More prayer, more serving, more giving, more journaling. None of it was working. Nothing seemed to feed my soul like before. And with every crashing wave of emotion came questions: *How can someone who loves God and serves Him experience such suffering? God, oh God, where are you? How can you leave in my darkest hour?*

Silence is all I heard.

Lost in a swirl of grief, I stood washing dishes night after night, longing for the ache of loss to lessen. Longing for a place for my soul to find rest. A place lived loved. A place where grace won instead of guilt. A place where celebration replaced comparison. A place where shame and the whispers of past mistakes disappeared in a sea of endless grace. A place where my identity was not in what I did but in a deep knowing of who I am in Christ. I longed for God to wrap me in His arms and tell me, "Everything will be okay." I wanted a place to exhale and finally rest from the constant attempt to heal myself. But instead, I had no idea what to do with my pain.

I imagined myself truly free in Christ, trusting Him with the future, learning to be deeply okay with where I am on my journey, even if it looks nothing like my neighbors. *What if all our activities only mask our insecurities?* What if masking the hurts interrupts the healing God is trying to do? I wanted God to move tangibly because I'm tired of pretending I'm okay.

In the grip of loss and trauma, suffering shines a giant spotlight on your human condition—no more fake smiles. No more brushing the hurt under the rug. No more white-knuckling my way through grief. No more numbing the pain. No more hiding behind the mask of "I'm okay." It's time to get real and raw.

During this silent period, I wrestled with some heavy theology. I asked the Lord many questions about what Christianity should look like. Slowly, God untangled the lies I believed and replaced them with His truth, and as He did, I felt a new woman beginning to emerge. Slowly, the woman deep within me that had always been there came out, a woman buried within the heaviness of grief, heartache, betrayal, loss, and considerable disappointment. A woman who one day learned how to feel all her emotions, allowing them to co-exist, letting them bubble to the surface rather than stuffing them down to keep up that good Christian appearance. This new woman that God brought out learned it's better to feel and be vulnerable than hide behind a smile. She now knows it's much better to be her most authentic self, even if she is no longer welcome at the same tables as she was before. God did something new within me, and I exhaled, allowing Him to do the work.

Though it's been three years, I'm still healing and learning what it means to be loved unconditionally in a world that loves you for what you produce rather than who you are.

While I was washing dishes one night, God broke the silence with an invitation: *"Lea, I know your suffering feels like punishment, but it's not; it's an invitation to more of me."*

Several days later, I read a familiar parable Jesus told in a new way:

*"A man was going down from Jerusalem to Jericho and fell into the hands of robbers. They stripped, beat him up, and fled, leaving him half dead. A priest happened to be going down that road. When he saw him, he passed by on the other side. In the same way, a Levite, when he arrived at the place and saw him, passed by on the other side. But a Samaritan approached him on his journey, and when he saw the man, he had compassion. He went over to him and bandaged his wounds, pouring on olive oil and wine. Then he put him on his own animal, brought him to an inn, and cared for him. The next day, he took out two denarii, gave them to the innkeeper, and said, "Take care of him. When I come back, I'll reimburse you for whatever extra you spend"* –Luke 10:30-35.*

As I read this scripture, Jesus spoke to my spirit, saying, "I am the Samaritan, and you are the wounded man. Allow me to heal you. I know you feel overlooked and small, but I see your pain. So allow me to minister to your heart by pouring compassion and kindness on you. Trust me with your pain. And when your wounds are no longer raw, I'll release you to minister to others. People may say, 'Get over it,' but I'm calling you to more. Have patience because the journey may seem long as we walk through this valley together."

I'm taken aback. Even though I was in so much pain, just like the man from Jerusalem, it seemed as if others overlooked my grief. Everyone forgets those in pain in a rush to check all the practical boxes, and sometimes, the person we're forgetting is ourselves. It always seems easier to numb than feel. Little do we know that if we keep burying how we feel, we'll bury ourselves alive.

God knows we need rescuing.

*Lea, do you trust me?*

I sat with the question for a long time. Did I trust God with my suffering and pain? Is it even faith if I only trust Him when life is easy? Would He be trustworthy in the dark valleys of despair?

*"Even though I walk through the valley of the shadow of death, I will fear no evil, for you are with me; your rod and staff comfort me."* (Psalm 23:4)

This is a verse many of us have etched in our hearts as a promise from

God. It encourages many of us not to succumb to fear even in the darkest valley, where death's presence looms, and the grip of anxiety tightens. In those moments of despair, God is by our side, providing comfort and peace through His unwavering presence.

When death steals and cancer rots, when our story takes a turn for the worse, and we collapse on the floor in tears, barely hanging on because it's all too much to bear, God commits to walk *through* it with us, never letting go of our hands.

Our job is to take time to heal and allow God to minister to our hearts. Often, we find ourselves striving to be strong for those around us, pouring out our love and support without reserving any for ourselves. Setting aside time for healing can seem impossible, as if it would take away from the needs of others.

In his book *Soul Keeping,* John Ortberg writes, "What do we do in the dark night? We do nothing. We wait. We remember that we are not God. We hold on. We ask for help. We do less. We resign from things, and we rest more. We stop attending church and ask somebody else to pray because we can't. We let go of our need to hurry through it. You can't run in the dark."[6]

That's a tall order to fill in a world continuing to spin with people who keep on going no matter what.

It takes a whole new level of faith to trust Jesus to minister to our wounds. Are we willing to slow down long enough for Him to care for us? Can we genuinely believe that He cares for our unseen hurts? Can we find the courage to trust Him?

Sometimes, we find ourselves stripped of all self-determination, empty of the familiar practices of praise, worship songs, gratitude journals, and comforting messages we've heard preached. Questioning God's presence in those moments and the grief along with it overwhelms us. It engulfs every fiber of our being, making us believe that this unbearable pain is our permanent reality.

What if this journey is the way forward? What if it's about something

---

[6] Ortberg, *Soul Keeping,* 183.

other than reaching a specific endpoint or doing everything perfectly? What if it's not about finding a formula to overcome or cope with grief and trauma? Because the truth is, there is no simple coping mechanism or five-step program that can neatly guide us out of the depths of our pain. There's no map with clear directions to follow. Instead, grief becomes intertwined with who we are. It becomes a constant companion, walking alongside us on this journey. It takes great courage to trust the slow process of grief.

So, instead of racing to get somewhere or fix something, we must learn to embrace grief as a part of our story. We must allow grief to shape, teach, and deepen our understanding of life and love. It's not about rushing through the process but finding the strength to navigate each step with faith, knowing Jesus is right there with us, offering His presence, comfort, and healing touch.

Arriving is not the point. It's not about following a five-step program to escape suffering or overcome trauma. It's about something more profound—keeping time with the One who created you, allowing God to love you in those deep places of pain.

In this place of feeling stuck, where despair takes hold, God invites us to embark on a new journey. A journey with an unknown destination. A journey that transcends physical places and material accomplishments because our ultimate destination is not a thing but a person—Jesus.

God never intended for us to feel the anguish of death and loss. Yet, with intricate emotions, our souls bear the weight of post-fall suffering. Our culture may not understand how to navigate these complex emotions, but we must not dismiss them, for they are sacred. God offers us the freedom to feel and embrace the full spectrum of our emotions in His infinite wisdom.

In his book *Grace Disguised*, Gerald Sittser says: "The pain of loss is unrelenting. It stalks and chases until it catches us. It is as persistent as wind on the prairies, as constant as cold in the Antarctic, as erosive as a spring flood. It will not be denied, and there is no escape from it".[7]

---

[7] Gerald Sittser, *A Grace Disguised* (Grand Rapids: Zondervan, 2004), 59.

Our culture offers quick fixes and how-to guides to bypass or suppress our feelings. Even our Bibles seem like instruction manuals, a way to transform sadness into instant happiness. But grief and healing don't operate on a quick timeline. The more we buy into the false theology that following Jesus guarantees a pain-free existence, the more we overlook the significance of grief or treat it like a problem to be solved.

Where did we learn that following Jesus would grant us a life devoid of suffering? Jesus Himself tells us, *"I tell you the truth, you will weep and mourn while the world rejoices. You will grieve, but your grief will turn to joy"* (Psalm 30:5). He doesn't promise a pain-free journey; rather, He acknowledges the reality of grief. He invites us to embrace grief, walk through it, and ultimately discover joy on the other side.

In our pain, we can find peace in the words of Jesus. He sees our tears, hears our cries, and offers assurance that our grief will not last forever. While the world may celebrate, we may find ourselves in mourning. But in the depths of our despair, we hold onto the hope that sorrow will give way to joy.

Transformative journeys simply cannot be rushed or neatly packaged with a bow on top.

We must let go of the misconception that following Jesus guarantees a pain-free life and cling to the realization that grief is natural—even a healthy response to the pain and suffering of this world. However, walking *through* is the only way forward. I know it can feel vast, barren, and desolate, where very few things seem to grow, let alone thrive. I know your mind is foggy, causing you to question if you're losing it. Forgotten and lonely, you wonder if this wilderness is your new permanent address. It's nearly impossible to continue hoping for a better tomorrow.

I get it. I've been there. And still find myself there at times.

Through this journey, we must cling to this truth and never let it go: The place where we feel Him and experience His never-ending love the most is in the middle of pain and suffering. We are held by God, and even if we don't feel His embrace, His Presence will never leave. Those desolate places of hopelessness where we've cried out in prayer for years without answers are invitations for more of God. I've learned firsthand that God draws near in these hopeless places where silence looms.

Amidst my heartbreak, the hope I desperately needed came unexpectedly. My suffering became a birthplace for divine participation. Never could I have imagined God showing up in the darkest areas of my life as He did.

## The Invitation

Time stands still on this last humid, hot day of July. Just one day after the fire, we returned to what was once our home. It was startling to see over twenty years of life reduced to ash in just a few hours. Nothing seems to be able to settle my mind as we approach the ruins of our home. Anxiety rises with each step toward the side entrance of what's left of the building. I'll never forget the smell. Acrid and unpleasant. It jolted me out of my numbness. *Oh God, how could this have happened?*

Bearing the immense weight of devastation, we move cautiously through the wreckage, striving to assess the extent of the destruction. Every corner we turn reveals the ruthless reach of the fire. Suppressing our tears, we methodically inspect each room. Clothes that had been in the washing machine now lie as ash, and the once neatly hung clothes in the closet are reduced to cinders scattered across the floor.

As I enter the master bathroom, I'm taken aback by what unfolds before me. It's a moment where God's presence is palpable, a reminder of His unpredictable but ever-present love. Stepping into the room amidst the ashes, I'm greeted not by one but by several butterflies. Each delicate creature briefly lands on the charred remains before fluttering away to the next patch of debris. I'm overcome by the sight, sensing an indescribable feeling of hope and renewal wash over me.

It's as if God has orchestrated this surreal scene, sending these winged messengers to perform a silent dance before me. Their fleeting presence symbolizes the promise of new beginnings rising from the ashes of destruction. I commit this image to memory, knowing that even in the darkest moments, God's grace shines through in unexpected ways.

The butterflies are a powerful reminder of the gift of grace and hope. It's a breathtaking, holy, bewildering hallelujah during destruction. It's as if God is saying, "I'm still here, even if you don't always see the evidence of me working. I am here, and I'll bring beauty among the ashes."

*"Behold, I am doing a new thing; now it springs forth, do you not perceive it? I will make a way in the wilderness and rivers in the desert"*
(Isaiah 43:19).

In that moment, my heart attaches to His, allowing me to sing a broken hallelujah over the next few months. God is forever trying to connect with us, reminding us that we're not forging our way blindly but that He's already ordered our steps (Psalm 119:133). God's courting us with His lovingkindness to experience a deeper intimacy in suffering. It requires a profound trust, knowing He's making all things beautiful in His perfect timing. Traumatic events break you and remake you, and out of the ashes, a new life begins.

The sight of the butterflies triggers a vivid memory from several years ago, during prayer. I recall feeling anxious and demanding that God intervene in a specific situation. Instead, I received a different response: a mental image of Jesus standing in a garden, reaching out to hold my hand. As I grasp His hand, a sense of calm washes over me, and we begin to dance together.

Locked in a gaze with Him, I hear His reassuring words: "There's no need to worry about a thing; it's just you and me now. It's not about having all the answers but accepting the invitation to live in an intimate connection with Me."

Without intimacy with God, hope fades like shattered dreams, and we stop believing beauty will come among the ashes. So here's the thing: we don't need an attitude change or Christian clichés to help us think positively. We need our hearts connected to His.

Maybe you're like me and need to hear this: God can make something beautiful even out of the most vulnerable, broken areas of your life—through pain, waiting, wrestling, and difficulty, beauty can arise. I know it's hard to believe God is at work. We all want a happy ending without the painful journey. Yet it takes desperately holding onto His promises through the valley of pain to value the beauty among the ashes.

Barbara Brown Taylor writes, "Pain makes theologians of us all… Pain is one of the fastest routes to a no-frills encounter with the Holy."[8]

---

[8] *An Altar in the World* (New York: HarperOne, 2009), 157-58.

Suffering never leaves you the same. It opens your eyes, rearranges your theology, exposes the lies you once believed, and produces an awareness of God's presence.

Blinded by our harsh conditions and longing for a fairy tale ending, we can miss the intimacy God offers us. Believing nothing good comes from the wilderness strips us of all hope, causing us to despise the place God is inviting us into where we can encounter His presence. This is precisely the opposite of what the Bible presents; the wilderness can be hopeful and prosperous.

In his immense suffering, Job declared. *"My ears had heard of you before. But now my eyes have seen you."*[9] In the crucible of pain, our understanding of God expands, and we catch a glimpse of His glory previously hidden from us.

God invites us through our suffering to experience a deep, divine connection. Do you know what I love about invitations? They let someone know their presence is requested, wanted, and valued. Invitations are intentional and purposeful. Just like God desired a relationship with the Israelites in the wilderness, He desires a relationship with us. As we journey onward, we'll experience God and His character in new ways.

This invitation extended to us in the wilderness of grief isn't one we might desire. Yet, throughout Scripture, we see God not only meeting people in the wilderness but inviting them to experience his goodness to a greater measure than those on an easy path. The Israelites, Elijah, Hagar, Moses, John the Baptist, the woman at the well, and even Jesus encountered God in their suffering.

You may ache, and no one may seem to understand or care.

You appear to be keeping a composed exterior, but inside, you're struggling not to unravel, fearing that if you let yourself feel, you might completely break down. If the tears start, they may never stop.

There's one truth I hang on to: if God met people where they were all those years ago in the Bible, He'll meet us where we are today. He sees you. He knows you. He loves you. He wants you to feel your feelings.

---

[9] Job 42:5 NCV

He wants you to heal from the inside out. He sees and hears your pain.

Today, He's inviting us to stop numbing the pain and allow Him to heal the brokenness. We don't need to hide the pain from the One who heals. Avoiding and numbing our feelings will lead us down an even darker path. Everything we go through leads us somewhere: either we lean into the discomfort or lean away. God promises if we lean towards it, He will meet us with hope.

However, letting the emotions arise requires a new level of surrender, no longer attempting to protect ourselves from pain. We think time heals, but time only hides and subdues the pain. Jesus is the only One who heals!

We must be gentle with ourselves as we trust Him with our brokenness. We must free ourselves to feel, grieve, and heal. As we continue to navigate the depths of our pain, may we discover the profound joy that can emerge from the darkest sorrows.

I pray we allow Him to wrap our wounds and pour His oil of gladness over us. And I pray we let go of the lie that it's selfish to take time to be with Jesus to heal. He waits, wanting to take care of us. Remember, we can only pour out blessings for others if we allow Him to minister to us.

Allow His Presence to wash away all guilt as we hear Him say, *"Arise, my darling. Come away, my beautiful one"* (Song of Songs 2:10).

Dear friend, allow the pain to be your compass to keep walking; your promise is waiting.

## DIGGING DEEPER:

1. Have you ever considered that your experience of loss and grief could be an opportunity to encounter God in a new and transformative way?
2. Are you willing to embrace the pain and allow it to be a catalyst for deepening your relationship with God, even if it means embarking on a journey that may change your life? Write openly about how you feel after reading this chapter.

# CHAPTER 3

## IT'S OKAY TO FEEL

*"Don't close off any part of yourself from Me. I know you inside and out, so do not try to present a "cleaned-up" self to Me."*
*– Sarah Young* [10]

Ten days after the fire, I stare at the ceiling of our rental home, feeling like my head is too heavy to lift. I lie there, hearing the kids in the kitchen getting ready for school, knowing I need to get up. Everything is an effort, even getting out of bed. Tears come without warning as I think: How will we move forward? How will I live life when suffering finds me again and again?

Looking out the window, I see the garbage truck taking our trash. How are people going about their day as if nothing happened? Don't they know?

I am not sleeping deeply. Night after night, my mind spins. I jar awake, terrified, trying to make sense of it all. They say it's the most extensive fire our town has ever seen. Five fire stations from surrounding towns merge to tame the flames. We lost everything. I sob over losing old journals and Bibles. I kept them in a basket on a bottom shelf, thinking my grandchildren might read them one day. You never know what you'll grieve till it's gone.

---

10 Sarah Young, *Jesus Calling* (Nashville: Thomas Nelson, 2004), 28.

I peel myself out of bed, whispering, *God, give me strength.* Those whisper prayers are what keep my heart beating with His.

I am thankful for friends who step in to help prepare the children for school. They repeatedly wrap me in love by dropping uniforms off with brand-new iPads, delivering school supplies to our doorstep, and preparing dinners each night. People saw a need and met it.

After dropping the children off at school, tears kept coming as I sat alone outside for the first time since the fire. I hear the water running upstairs as my oldest daughter showers. Ten days just are not enough time when you've experienced a traumatic event, so I allow her to stay home during that first week of school. So many questions rush through my mind. I feel bruised and tender. I know I need to hear from God because I have no idea how to walk through this.

Each day drags into the next. I keep attempting to preach God's goodness to my soul in any way I can. Notecards line the mirror with verses reminding me that He never leaves or forsakes us. Brain fog clouds the truth of His word. *Is God really good?*

I do everything to run toward His goodness and not away from it. It's a miracle I don't shut down from sheer exhaustion. My regular reading of the Word shines a light in the darkness in my mind, even if it's only one verse. I feel as if I am holding onto the corner of His cloak, doing everything I can not to let go.

The ordinary everyday moments are too much to bear. Throwing in the laundry. Making the bed. Taking out the trash. Feeding the kids and making sure I eat, too. Taking a short walk to the mailbox. Meeting with the insurance agent. Picking up the kids. Doing the homework. It all bumps up against the raging war inside my head, which I later discover is grief. I am going through the motions, unable to navigate how I feel, which causes me to lash out and spew hurtful words to the ones I love.

The chain of events breaks me down over the next year. My family is ushered into season after season of surprising trauma. As I do everything I can to keep our family from breaking and avoiding further suffering, God mends the broken pieces into something beautiful.

I realize I'm not alone. After loss or trauma, many people navigate a wilderness of emotions and cannot make sense of it all. We find ourselves sweeping up broken pieces of our shattered lives despite our efforts to avoid it.

I've heard from many of you.

A private message arrives, asking for prayers as Mary finalizes her divorce. Christmas is quickly approaching, and she doesn't know what she will do without the house full of laughter and squeals from her kids.

My friend Rachel calls to tell me that her husband's life insurance is dropping him because he has stage-four cancer. He is only 40 years old, and they have three small children.

A text from Deb asking for prayers for her daughter caught in addiction who is in the hospital detoxing because the police found her.

Over coffee, Jen weeps while telling me they've tried everything, and the doctors tell them there is nothing further to do; she will not be able to give birth.

Christy and Matt's marriage is dissolving. The more they go to counseling, the worse it seems to get. Finally, they both settle that their marriage is not what they expected.

Mindy confides that her son is expelled from school again for smoking marijuana in the boy's bathroom.

I sit in Bible study as Cindy reveals her sadness and struggles as a forty-year-old single woman. She thought for sure she would be married by now.

Lillian's husband's drinking has gotten out of hand, and he finally checks himself into rehab, but two affairs and endless arguing in front of the kids have already caused too much damage.

I stand grieving with a friend who suddenly loses her fifty-two-year-old husband, and time seems to stop. Twelve hours ago, they sat, had dinner, and kissed each other good night. No one warned her that the hands of the clock would suddenly stop her marriage.

My phone rang, and my friend tells me her husband flipped his car, and they're rushing him to the emergency room. He had a stroke at only fifty. Life will be forever changed for their family.

The stories feel endless. These are real people with real-life, unexpected heartaches and disappointments. They all experienced grief from loss or trauma, but some didn't even realize it.

Christians can repress and avoid hard feelings by overemphasizing the positive and rejoicing always. There's a term for this kind of faith: spiritual bypassing. In the 1980s, John Welwoo defined spiritual bypassing as using "spiritual ideas and practices to sidestep personal emotional 'unfinished business,' to shore up a shaky sense of self, or to belittle basic needs, feelings, and developmental tasks."[11]

Just today, I received an email from a woman confessing she hasn't found another person to talk to about the pain of her husband's chronic illness. Another woman suffering from infertility says I'm the only person she's confided in besides her husband.

People are suffering alone because they are embarrassed by how they feel.

We never talk about how we only make room for warm, fuzzy emotions while the hard emotions loom in the background. We need to begin telling our stories and allowing space for each other to feel. The first step is naming the feeling after loss and trauma grief and then holding space for it. This is Biblical: *"And He took with him Peter, James, and John, and began to be greatly distressed and troubled. And He said to them, "My soul is very sorrowful, even to death"* (Mark 14:33-34).

Jesus named His emotions and gave them space in His friends' presence. Pretending painful things don't hurt is not being courageous; admitting that painful things hurt is. Healing deep wounds without a scar is not our story; neither was Jesus's.

---

[11] Craig S. Cashwell, Harriet L. Glosoff, and Chereé Hammond, "Spiritual Bypass: A Preliminary Investigation," *Counseling and Values* 54, no. 2 (April 2010): 162–74, https://doi.org/10.1002/j.2161-007x.2010.tb00014.x.

## The Dark Nights

Rather than feel the hurt and pain, we wish it away. When we long for the dark nights to be gone forever, we are actually longing for God to show up in our midst.

We feel loved, seen, and held with one glimpse of His glorious face. Isn't that what anyone wants, to not feel alone?

But I didn't feel held and certainly didn't feel loved. For months, the unpredictability and fickleness of my emotions left me feeling helpless one minute and angry the next. Taming the voices swirling in my mind and the whispering lies seemed impossible.

My oldest daughter no longer stays at home without an adult. How can I help her see that God will protect her when she feels abandoned? What does it even mean for God to protect us? People die each day believing God will protect them. How do I look her in the eye and say, "God will protect you," when she stood alone months earlier with her three younger siblings, watching her home be consumed in flames? What if God doesn't spare their lives when the next traumatic event happens? What if she never heals from this event? What if I discover that the God I've served all these years doesn't honor His promises?

These questions are scary. The only way to calm my mind is by scrolling through social media, admiring and sometimes envying the lives of others. I stay up late watching Netflix and wake up just in time to take the kids to school. On some awful nights, I admit I drink too many cocktails. Okay, not some nights, many nights. I'm not drinking to be social. I drink to stop the roaring thoughts and questions. I'm running away from the stillness, and I'm completely lost.

One day, when we are alone in the car, my husband asks, "Why are you crying?" Tears flow down my cheeks randomly during the day without warning, as if my grief just has to seep out.

His simple question completely unzips me. I spill my heart out, holding nothing back. It feels honest and raw.

Don't Ignore Your Feelings

I tell my husband I've had it all wrong. I misunderstand what it means to be strong. When the pain comes rushing in, instead of permitting myself to feel it, I tell myself, "You must be strong for the children."

I deny my feelings in an attempt to hold our life together. If I'm numb, I won't feel. If I don't feel, I can move on as if nothing happened... except the grief seeps out in rage and extreme sadness.

Guilt weighs on me for feeling this way. Our culture prefers us to place a polite facade over our dark emotions.

As I pour out my heart, my husband, Mike, pours out his, admitting he never grieved his father's death. It's been twenty-two years since his father's death, and Mike finally realizes his built-up anger and resentment are from his lack of grieving. He believed the same lie I had: if he keeps moving forward, the sadness will magically dissolve. He felt like he didn't have much choice.

Several months after his father's passing, he started medical school and joined the military, and if that wasn't enough, we were navigating the difficulties that come from being newly married. Unfortunately, his dad died only six weeks after our wedding. At only twenty-one years old, he felt like his only option was to stuff the sadness and pain down, he looked like he had it all together on the outside, yet he was dying on the inside. For twenty years, he ignored the warning signs of stress and discomfort in determination to keep going. Mike, for all those years, ran on anxiety, always one minute away from a breaking point, often erupting in anger over minor inconveniences.

For years, he's tried everything to manage his stress, changing and tweaking his schedule to make more time for rest. Little did he know that not taking the time to grieve his dad's death meant other underlying issues would go unresolved. His lack of grieving cost him years of anger and bitterness. Our family enduring our own three years of grief and pain caused him to realize the anger and resentment stemming from his lack of healing. Mike slowly became less angry and bitter as he processed and gave himself time to grieve.

There's a myth about men that our culture adopts as truth, and my husband is no exception. Men, at young ages, are conditioned not to show emotion. It's not considered manly, and they must white-knuckle their way through pain and grief, minimizing how they genuinely feel.

As a result, men learn to ignore their feelings and push through the pain to move on.[12] This myth applies to women as well.

The truth is that hurt people hurt people, and I see this in my husband and myself. We have to feel the hurt to heal the wound. We have to find a place for our negative feelings. If we don't, they will rule our lives and our families.

Most of us grew up ignoring our emotions. Along the way, we've adopted the mindset that following Christ looks like skipping through a field of flowers with a smile on our faces, and if you felt any different, you must be out of God's will. So, we do the only logical thing: we rise above them. Instead of being authentic and honest with each other, we slap a pretend smile on and say things like, "God's got this."

I'm here to say it's not only okay to feel; we must feel to heal. Moving forward takes awareness of the body, mind, soul, and spirit. Ignoring and stuffing our feelings costs us precious time and never makes things right.

Being angry and sad are human emotions felt even by Jesus. So when pain and loss happen, allow yourself to grieve. Let go of the expectations to feel a certain way. What you're walking through is complex, and the last thing you need to do is stuff your feelings, ignoring them as if that is the more spiritual way to handle them. The way to wholeness begins by giving words to your emotions. God created our emotions. He loves us no more and no less because of them.

As my husband and I return home after that conversation in the car, I sit on our bed in the rental home and allow the feelings to rush over me.

I love what Sue Monk Kidd says in her book *When the Heart Waits*: "God created my emotions, my instincts, my senses, and my body as well as my spirit and my mind—and pronounced them all good."[13]

I once heard a wonderful illustration regarding emotions in a sermon. The pastor referred to our feelings as a check engine light on

---

12 Miriam Greenspan, *Healing Through the Dark Emotions: The Wisdom of Grief, Fear, and Despair* (United Kingdom: Shambhala, 2004).
13 HarperOne, October 11, 2016.

a car warning us if something is wrong. When the check engine light blinks in our vehicle, it causes us to pay attention and investigate why it blinks. The blinking indicates the car needs attention. Our emotions are like a check engine light for our minds and hearts. They indicate that they need attention. Emotions are information.

Several years ago, I got a call from a friend asking if I could pick her up and take her to a nearby gas station since her car stalled several miles from my house. Her lack of paying attention to the car needing gas caused an inconvenience to her day.

It's strange how we think ignoring warning signs is best. We may think we're saving time, but it will only cost us.

Ignoring "negative" emotions, such as grief, fear, or sadness, for long enough can turn into hopelessness, despair, and bitterness. Feeling and processing our emotions is our avenue to becoming unstuck.

*Ding, ding, ding!* Something is not right, and it's time to pay attention.

Several years ago, I volunteered at an addiction rehab. Each week, I sat in a room with women who had numbed their emotions with drugs and alcohol for years. Not one of them had a decent father. Their baby daddies were in and out of jail. Most came from poverty, with young moms who also abused drugs and alcohol. They saw no earthly idea of escaping the pain except through, you guessed it, drugs and alcohol. These women were assigned to meet with me to learn how to tend to their souls.

I prayed they would feel the Father's love each week and open up to another way of coping with life. Despite the horrible circumstances they had encountered, I prayed they would succeed. They had a lot of work to do, walking through the shadow of death and feeling all the complex emotions they had numbed for years.

Their addictions buried their feelings. They thought if they didn't feel their emotions, they wouldn't exist. But here they all were, forced to stare those feelings in the face and grieve their losses. I remember sitting there amongst these women struggling to break the cycle of addiction and knowing I wasn't going to teach them as much as they were going to teach me.

For the first time in years, these deeply broken women were choosing to face their pain without drugs. What bravery.

While we may not be abusing drugs and alcohol, we most likely are numbing our emotions through overly busy schedules, food, screen time, acceptable pills, games, shopping… anything to escape the pain. But what would happen if we stepped back and took inventory of our souls? The truth is, underneath those raw emotions are some lies we've come to believe, and without tending to our feelings, we'll never acknowledge our need for Truth.

During my time at the rehab center, one day, I asked a few of the women to share their stories. One by one, each woman voiced how their addiction started. None of them woke up one morning intending to ruin their lives. Instead, they each had an awful trigger point, causing them to turn to drugs. With tears, I looked into their eyes. I felt their pain. I told them, "You are so brave and courageous for being here."

Every time we choose to show up to better ourselves, we are being *courageous*.

After class, I called my sister-in-law and cried. I didn't believe I had anything to offer these women. What do I know about drug and alcohol abuse? (Little did I know that I would know way more than I wanted in just a few years.) After voicing my frustrations about not being enough, my sister-in-law said something profound: "I think religion makes us think we always have to fix someone or teach them something. What if it's about just showing up and holding space for them to heal?"

"Hold space for them?" I asked. "What does that mean?"

Holding space is ministry. Ministry is simply loving like Jesus. Ministry means loving the person in front of you, and sometimes, the person in front of you… is you.

Maybe it's time we hold space for ourselves.

We can't afford to neglect taking care of our souls. David spoke truth to himself: *"Find rest, O my soul, in God alone"* (Psalm 62:1,5).

We live unawakened when we neglect our souls.

Today, I can apply this principle of holding space for myself.

Giving yourself time and space to feel is not only healthy, it's also Biblical. Look at David in Psalm 22. David, the man after God's own heart, penned this scripture passage questioning God's being very real and honest with His emotions: *"My God, I cry by day, but You do not answer, by night, yet I have no rest"* (Psalm 22:2). Sound like words we say? *God, where are you?* I'm so grateful for the honesty in Scripture. *"I am a worm and not a man, scorned by men and despised by people. Everyone who sees me mocks me"* (Psalm 22:6-7)—pure honesty before God.

There's no protecting ourselves from suffering. You can't numb it away. Pray it will disappear. Or ignore it. It will still be there, waiting for you to feel it.

The thing is, only you can do the hard work. And it starts with holding space for yourself. And maybe, just maybe, you'll wake up one day and realize all this pain and suffering has made you more loving and compassionate.

| **DIGGING DEEPER:** |
| --- |
| 1. How are you doing today? Really? Consider taking the next few minutes to think about how you are coping. Write honestly in your journal. |
| 2. Could you envision your grief becoming a sacred journey leading to a profound encounter with God, ultimately transforming your life? |

# CHAPTER 4

## OPEN HEART SURGERY

*In times of upheaval, a voice from heaven says, 'Be still and know that I am God.' It doesn't say, 'Be still and know why.' In a distant day, the gradual sacrament of understanding may be offered to us."* [14]

Darkness loomed over us as we walk hand-in-hand into the Alabama Children's Hospital one fateful Friday morning. Another heart surgery awaited our eleven-year-old son Elijah on the other side of those doors. We were pretty anxious people by now. We were accustomed to our lives falling apart.

At our son's pre-op appointment, the surgeon reassured us his hospital stay would be about a week, though rare complications could make it longer. However, we're praying for a quick, easy recovery. This warrior son of mine has already endured two heart surgeries. Half a heart doesn't keep beating on its own. Thank God this kid's heart is still beating longer than expected.

God, in all His mercies, gave our son the best surgeon in the nation, and with God's healing power, he performed two experimental heart surgeries. Almost ten years separated those first two surgeries, the first

---

[14] H. Norman Wright, *Experiencing Grief* (United States: Broadman & Holman, 2004), 30.

performed when he was just four days old, the second at seven months old.

Eleven years ago, I sat for the first time in a stale hospital room with flickering fluorescent lights, listening to the beeping sounds of machines keeping Elijah alive, and now here I am again.

It all started with an email from our adoption agency asking if we'd adopt a baby with a severe heart defect. Unknowingly, years later, I'd be sitting in the ICU staring anxiously at my son with a wired-shut chest and tubes running everywhere, wondering why he had to be the one with the rare complication.

A week-long hospital stay turns into four weeks. You can't prepare mentally for a month of sleeping next to your son in a makeshift bed that feels like a pile of rocks while never leaving his side except to grab coffee or lunch. Yet, here you are with unexpected moments of grace, the two of you spending uninterrupted quality time together.

Being two hours away from home with one of the five children isn't easy. Especially since my oldest is spiraling out of control and needs me home, and my husband is exhausted from working and driving two hours back and forth. My mother-in-law can only do so much to hold down the fort while caring for four kids.

Why in the world does suffering come in waves? One thing after *another often happens with no breath in between. What if this isn't the last unexpected stop in this wilderness of grief? What if I wither away in the land of suffering, never to return?*

I was tired of it all.

I was tired of praying. Tired of fighting. Tired of believing. How could it all work out? Life can feel overly complicated when you're grieving and hurting.

*Will it all be okay? Will my heart ever stop hurting from the pain of it all?*

I fumble with my words, attempting to explain to my son with yet another chest tube why we were still in this place. They can't seem to find a way to keep fluid from building up in his lungs without the chest tubes inserted. Pulling and reinserting them three times is disheartening. My heart hurt to see my son go through such pain.

"I don't think I can take this," I said to my husband one Saturday when he visited.

"Except for the fluid build-up around the lungs, his heart is healing," he responded with tenderness, knowing how hard this has been.

*But what about my heart?*

I spend these weeks with more than enough time to examine my soul. An extended hospital stay can undoubtedly do that. I try to come face to face with the pain and deep disappointment with how life has gone, knowing I need to stop numbing my emotions. Trauma and loss cause me to pull away and not trust God, once again questioning the theology I have believed my whole life.

Maybe you've lost a loved one or your home. Perhaps your loss isn't as tangible. Maybe it's a trauma you've kept buried, a bandage hiding an open wound. You've struggled to understand it, not knowing how to feel—gasping for air and unsure how to move forward. The pain pulls you under, you've got more questions than answers, and you're afraid to admit it, but you wonder, *where is God?*

With each day rolling into the next, holding onto your to-do list with one hand and concealing a hemorrhaging wound with the other feels complicated. Your expectations of what life should look like doesn't align with reality.

Navigating the complexities of life while concealing a deep, hemorrhaging wound can be overwhelming. Our expectations for what life should look like collide with the stark reality before us, engulfing us in a wave of sadness.

Unlike natural losses, unexpected wounds and suffering bring additional complexity as our lives rearrange, and intense grief pierces our souls. We find ourselves wandering through a dark and unfamiliar terrain, grasping for understanding.

This is what experts call ambiguous loss.

Ambiguous loss, a term coined by family therapist Dr. Paul Boss forty years ago, aptly captures the essence of this emotion. It is a loss without closure, an ongoing trauma where answers seem elusive. The pieces of our shattered reality lie scattered, each bearing jagged edges that leave us questioning what went wrong. We find ourselves adrift in a sea of ambiguity, unsure how to navigate the depths of our emotions.[15]

In our culture, ambiguous loss is often misunderstood and overlooked. This kind of loss doesn't have a grief or support group because it doesn't fit into traditional narratives. We grapple with mixed emotions, unsure of how to feel. It is a lonely and disorienting experience; the support and understanding of others may be absent due to its unique nature.

But let me tell you that amidst the confusion and isolation. Even in the darkest corners of our grief, there is a path to healing and restoration. It starts with acknowledging the reality of our loss, embracing the complexity of our emotions, and seeking support from those who can journey with us through the ambiguity. By understanding our experience is valid and deserves care, we can begin to navigate this uncharted territory with grace and resilience.

If you're grappling with ambiguous loss, know you are not alone. Your pain is real, and your journey is significant. Together, let us explore the depths of our emotions, hold space for the complexity of our grief, and discover the healing that comes from acknowledging and honoring our unique experiences of loss.

The difficulty is that healing doesn't happen until you feel the deep pain of grief. We don't get over loss and trauma. We work hard at it, though. We read books, go to therapy, drink water, say prayers, go to church, sing songs, and the list continues. We try.

But the scars remain. And we become humbled and shocked by the reality that our desired outcomes don't match our efforts.

The divorce happens. Addiction continues to rip through families. Jobs are lost. Cancer plays no favorites. Personalities change. Relationships

---

[15] Pauline Boss, "Ambiguous Loss Theory: Challenges for Scholars and Practitioners," *Family Relations* 56, no. 2 (March 22, 2007): 105–11, https://doi.org/10.1111/j.1741-3729.2007.00444.x.

grow apart. Wombs stay empty. Despite our best efforts, suffering, pain, and disappointments still rear their ugly heads.

### Jesus Chooses to Walk Among the Sick

There was once a pool called Bethesda where disabled people sat around, not just any body of water, but one with healing powers. People believed an angel periodically came down from heaven to stir the water, and healing came to the first one in the pool.

One day, Jesus walks through Jerusalem and comes upon a pool surrounded by people around the water's edge. Imagine Jesus, full of compassion, closely examining each person there.

Jesus walks among the suffering.

Picture it: wounded, desperate people surround this pool. Most of them sit there day in and day out, maybe even hungry, and most wear the same clothes for months. I bet it smells, and healthy people never even consider strolling by the pool. Yet Jesus comes right up to the water. God draws near to our brokenness, not just our faith or righteousness alone. Nine times, the gospels declare Jesus moves with compassion: "*He heals the brokenhearted and binds up their wounds*" (Psalm 147:3).

He could have been anywhere that day, but he chose to walk among the sick. As he walks, he spots a man. Because Jesus never does anything without a purpose, I wonder if he approaches this man knowing he's been sick for thirty-eight years—that's a long time to suffer.

"*Jesus asked him, 'Do you want to get well?'*

*'Sir, I have no one to put me into the pool when the water is stirred. While I am trying to get in, someone else goes down ahead of me.'*

*Then Jesus said to him, 'Get up! Pick up your mat and walk.' At once, the man was cured; he picked up his mat and walked*" (John 5:5-9).

*Sound familiar?*

The man replied similarly to how we might have: "*'Sir, I have no one to put me into the pool when the water is stirred. While I am trying to get in, someone else goes down ahead of me.'*"

Why on earth does Jesus ask a man who has been disabled for thirty-eight years if he wants to be well? Of course, he does. Why else would he be sitting by a healing pool? If you were this suffering man, how would you answer? Maybe something like, "I've been trapped in a body for thirty-eight years that doesn't work properly. I am tormented daily, wondering why everyone else receives healing while I'm stuck here without help. I'm sick of being sick. I've tried everything, and nothing works, and you're asking me if I want to be well. Can't you tell I do?"

After thirty-eight years of suffering, he didn't expect healing.

I've heard sermons criticizing this poor man for his lack of faith, conveying a message to those suffering to stop complaining, buck up, and not allow circumstances to define them. Of course, there are some elements of truth, such as the fact that circumstances don't determine who we are and that we shouldn't stay in a state of complaining. However, as we have learned, bypassing the heart of the matter will only further isolate and keep us stuck—pretending, pulling up our bootstraps, and ignoring our reality further deepens the lie that wholeness is synonymous with denying our pain.

However, when you examine this scripture through the lens of love and kindness that is characteristic of Jesus, you can see denying our pain is not God's intention for us. What if we changed our perspective? What if instead of bringing our complaints to others, we bring them to God, which becomes an act of worship?

This man sitting by the pool trusted God with his deepest pain, which became his greatest sacrifice. He's rendering complete control to Jesus.

Jesus's questions are not to shame us but to draw us into intimacy with Him. He didn't ask the people listening in on the conversation, "Why has no one helped this man?" Jesus, who sacrificed and saved us all, didn't jump to accusing others or defining the man by his condition.

There he was, feeling anxious, frustrated, desperate, helpless, and a bit vulnerable as Jesus approached. Knowing all this, Jesus asked, "Do you want to be well?" awakening the man to the possibility of healing. At the poolside, Jesus looked beyond the man's condition and looked at the man for who he was in his soul.

Everything in life is about developing a relationship with God. As the years turned into decades, I'm sure this man began questioning God's goodness, wondering if God even cared about him. In the everyday suffering and longing for things to be different, he couldn't see the One who comforts. Prolonged pain and suffering leaves you wounded and alone, paralyzed by grief.

After dedicating years of tirelessly adhering to rules and striving with all his might to muster faith for healing, the man by the pool found himself uncertain about what to do next. Then Jesus approached him with loving kindness to comfort his pain and suffering. He didn't sweep the pain and suffering under the rug. Jesus welcomed the man back into the relationship by stepping into the man's nightmare.

*"Then Jesus said to him, 'Get up! Pick up your mat and walk.'"*

If we examine Jesus's words, Jesus used the Greek word *hugios,* which means "made whole."

Suffering for thirty-eight years, the man needed more than healing. He needed *wholeness.* He needed to live intimately connected to the heart of the Father.

We all need wholeness. We need the touch of God. But, unfortunately, we forget to enjoy God's presence in our pursuit of finding relief from suffering.

For the man by the pool, it all started with an invitation: *Do you want to be made whole?*

When there's no end in sight of our pain and suffering, and we're exhausted, God extends mercy. Maybe our prayers sound something like this:

*I'm fine, God. I just have to keep moving, keep doing, stop crying. I'm better than this. I'm fine!*

God extends mercy and asks, *"But do you want to be made whole?"*

I wonder if the man hesitated. Sometimes, fear can dictate our response. It is much easier to continue moving through life than to feel.

Putting on our big girl pants seems easier than trusting God with all our disappointments and hurts. We discount our restlessness as a form of weakness. Marginalizing the extent of our pain dismisses the disappointment as unimportant. Our feelings are unreliable, or so we have been taught, so we throw them to the side, believing our pain is spiritually unnecessary. We underestimate the profound importance of dealing with and taking our emotions to the cross.

When we dismiss our feelings, we allow part of ourselves to die. Sometimes, the more difficult path is allowing ourselves to feel. God didn't merely come to save us from our sins. Jesus came to redeem all areas of our lives.

He came for us to walk in wholeness—body, mind, soul, and spirit.

I want to write it on the walls—I want to scream it from the rooftops: unattended, ongoing suffering and pain can develop into a deep wound, keeping us stuck in despair, depression, and bitterness.

No shame. No fear. No hiding. God's promise is abundant life. If we bleed alone without care, infection will set in, stealing our joy and peace.

When Jesus asks us if we want to be whole, He softly whispers, *"It's okay to feel. Come to me, and I will give you rest. What can I do for you? You can trust me with your hurts."*

Jesus steps into the pain and disappointment of the man's broken and fractured life at the Bethesda pool. His story, and our story, will always have a witness in the presence of Jesus. We're wholly seen and known by a God madly in love with us.

Jesus even takes it a step further. He says, *"Get up, take up your bed, and walk."*

Healing takes work on our part. It takes choosing to get up and not stay where we are. This man had a choice: Would he believe Jesus and get up, or would he continue to sit by the pool?

To "get up," we have to admit we are wounded.

As a nurse, I love wound care—there's something about the sense of accomplishment when you see the wound get better through proper care. Here's the thing about wound care, though: you can't slap a bandage on a dirty wound because it risks infection. The same is true for grief and trauma. We can't slap some Bible verses over the pain and think it will automatically heal. Unfortunately, our fast-paced world has taught us always to find the "easy fix"—the quicker we deal with these complicated emotions, the faster we can move on with life.

It doesn't work that way, not in the emergency room or the emotional realm, either. Slapping faith on an open wound creates a breeding ground for isolation, depression, bitterness, anger, and unforgiveness. An injury needs cleansing and to be handled with care, sometimes rebandaging it daily for months to heal properly and to prevent infection.

Much of what our culture believes about grief has seeped into our own belief system, blurring the lines of what it means to grieve with hope. Telling someone always to find the good in life is not a healing response. It's not helpful—just like you wouldn't tell someone with an open wound to look for the bright side that at least it wasn't amputation or death! God created us to feel and to feel deeply, and that's okay.

While suffering, people with good intentions tell us to find the good in our losses. Is *this* the Christian wound care for those suffering? Romans 8:28 tells us that God always works things together for the good of those who love Him, but I wonder if we too quickly quote this verse to indulge in wishful thinking. Do we use it to avoid dealing with our wounds rather than trusting God?

Sweeping away the hurt by finding the good is not the answer. A positive attitude forced upon those suffering causes shame and isolation.

We can see through the Gospels that God provides a different path forward. Imagine Jesus looking the man in the pool in the eyes as he sits there suffering and says, "Look on the bright side!" Hearing that statement is even crazier than asking, *"Do you want to be well?"*

Unfortunately, the American church has given in to the "check your burdens at the door" mentality, making it difficult for us to admit we're wounded. Being honest and sharing our hurts is considered a sign of weakness because if we know Jesus, we shouldn't hurt or suffer… right?

Instead of being open about our pain, we lay near healing waters for decades, too embarrassed to admit we're wounded and need help.

Attempting to find the good in the pain unknowingly is damaging. The longer we pretend we're not wounded, the longer we stay wounded.

As a nurse, I can tell you that there are three categories of physical wounds: scrapes and abrasions, lacerations, and puncture wounds. Each type heals differently, and some take longer than others. Some wounds bleed longer than others. Some wounds leave a scar, while others may not. No two wounds are the same. The same is true for emotional wounds.

There simply is no one-size-fits-all grief journey.

The need to cleanse the wound for healing is what all wounds have in common. Infection and complications can and will occur if the injury is left uncleaned. Keeping the wound clean avoids further complications. Similarly, a lifetime of suffering and unattended pain can lead to infection of the mind and heart. Emotional pain and anger lead to bitterness, deception, and even faulty thinking.

And here's a big problem: the infected wound can sometimes injure someone else. Because, you know, *"hurt people, hurt people."* It's a medical truth as well as an emotional one!

If you listen to another person's story long enough, it's likely a story of woundedness. One wound led to another because they never stopped to heal and grieve. They were overwhelmed by looking for relief from pain. What if we all paused, grieved each wound, and confessed the pain instead of pretending everything was okay? I bet our lives would be different.

I bet we wouldn't become stuck in despair and depression while Jesus continues to call us to *"'get up.'"* Jesus isn't asking us to find the bright side! He's delivering much more than that—healing. Psalm 147:3 says, *"He heals the brokenhearted and binds up their wounds."* Praise God!

I have sat by my son's side in this hospital room for nearly four weeks. It is four weeks filled with pacing the halls and placing my trust in God in a completely new way. As I navigate the whirlwind of stress, these times truly test me. I feel like the man sitting by the pool, wounded by life. I have to ask myself, am I brave enough to be honest with God and trust Him with my deepest pain because Jesus is calling to me, *"get up"*?

Wrestling through complex emotions rather than stuffing becomes my form of worship. Jesus asks us to emerge from our disappointments and trust Him again for restoration. Feeling much like that Bethesda man, I find comfort in allowing others to go into the pool before me to seek healing. Yet Jesus comes up to me, and He asks, "Do you want to be made whole?"

In the stillness of the night in the hospital room, I ponder Jesus's question. I know He is beckoning me to more. Through prayer and reading His word, God untangles some knotted-up theology and reintroduces Himself to me. Revealing new aspects of His character allows me to trust Him more and find new grace and courage to overcome.

Grief feels like a wilderness since my dad's death, my mom's cancer diagnosis, the fire, and then four weeks in the hospital with my son. I feel lost and tossed around by the wind, one moment clinging to God's presence and then wondering where He went. Although I long for intimacy and closeness, grief blinds me.

Trauma and suffering falsely paint the picture that the wilderness is our forever home. Nancy Demoss Wolgemuth says, "Anything that makes me need Jesus is a blessing."[16]

In Matthew 5:3, Jesus says, *"Blessed are the poor in spirit, for theirs is the kingdom of heaven."* The poor in spirit are those dependent on Jesus, much like David when he hears the news of his son's death, "who gets up from the floor, washes his face and combs his hair, puts on a fresh change of clothes, then goes to the sanctuary and worships"[17]—so wounded, yet in need of God's presence.

*The poor in spirit* is like a child who falls, skins their knee, and runs

---

[16] *Choosing Gratitude* (Chicago: Moody Publishers, 2009).
[17] 2 Samuel 12:20-22 MSG

to their mom, pulling back their hand in trust, revealing the gushing wound. There's complete trust that their mom will handle the injury with care.

Near the end of Psalm 51, David wrote this: *"...you will not be pleased with a burnt offering. The sacrifices of God are a broken spirit; a broken and contrite heart, O God, you will not despise"* (Psalm 51:16-17). David trusted God with his pain and suffering, trusting God to take his wounded heart and remake it.

Just like a mom or a nurse in the ER, God extends tenderness to perform wound care.

Pretending you're not hurting isn't healing you; it's only breeding frustration and further spreading its poison. I'm learning to stop saying I'm okay and learning to surrender to God's intimacy. Rather than guarding my wounds in hopes they will go away, I offer them to God as an act of worship, trusting and believing that God will take care of me and my pain.

Letting go is scary. Yet, I know God wants me to trust Him, and for the first time, I did.

There's something sacred in trusting a God who never leaves or shies away from our pain. There's a comfort in knowing He walks with us in our suffering and pain. Today, as I write, I feel the Holy Spirit saying to you and me, "Trust me. Hand me your disappointments and hurts, and I will restore all lost."

*"Joy and gladness will overtake them, and sorrow and sighing will flee"* (Isaiah 35:10).

Just days later, the situation takes another turn for the worse. More fluid accumulates around Elijah's lungs, and the hope of being home for the Super Bowl is replaced with a new promise of discharge from the hospital the following week. So, once again, my husband leaves on Sunday evening, facing yet another week as a single dad, while I remain in the hospital room with a eleven-year-old, navigating the daily duties of a parent who wants her child to be well.

As my husband says goodnight, I can see the tiredness of a long, endless season of unexpected grief in his eyes.

Once again, tears form as I kiss him goodnight before he leaves for home. Life feels complicated and painful.

I have chicken wings delivered to us, and my son and I make new memories by watching the Super Bowl together in his hospital room. Trying to turn my disappointment around, I sit with God later that night. Tuning out the beeping of the machines in the too-familiar hospital room, I slowly underline two words: "*get up*" in Luke 5. It all starts to make more sense, and I journal, writing these words to myself:

"The suffering feels endless, but be kind to yourself and allow grace upon grace. God's not expecting anything from you. He's not mad or disappointed. He's madly in love with you, and His eyes shine affectionately toward you. So, hold space for yourself to feel like you do for others. Stop numbing the sadness with drinking and scrolling. Permit yourself to feel, and you'll be surprised by the healing that comes. I know it hurts like hell. And everything seems out of place. Trust the process. One day, you'll feel the sun on your face again and love from God in your heart."

What if we trust the One who walks among our suffering and pain and offers us wholeness? What if we lived as if we believed He's everything we need?

## DIGGING DEEPER:

1. In your grief and trauma, pause and listen to Jesus' question: "Do you want to be made whole?" Reflect on your willingness to trust Him again and embrace restoration. Allow others to walk alongside you in seeking healing, recognizing that community is vital in the journey.

2. Seek stillness and solitude to deepen your connection with God and uncover new aspects of His character. Embrace grace and courage as you navigate the wilderness of grief, knowing it is not your permanent dwelling. Trust that God is calling you out of the wilderness and offering a pathway to healing, wholeness, and intimacy with Him.

# CHAPTER 5

## THE REALITY

*Welcome to life, where Plan A transforms into Plan Z to transform you.*[18]

A few days after the fire, I wrote in my journal, "Our family will prosper. We are not victims of a fire." I circle it several times to convince my heart to believe it.

I then write these words: "Even when the enemy comes in and seems to take everything—have no fear; our God redeems." "*After Job had prayed for his friends, the Lord restored his fortunes and gave him twice as much as he had before*" (Job 42:10).

It has been three years since writing those words, and I'm still waiting for God to restore all we lost. There are areas where He surprised us with complete restoration, but we're still waiting in faith for more.

Waiting makes me feel like my six-year-old daughter, who recently brought home a small cup of dirt, declaring, "Something beautiful is going to grow!" Every morning since, she springs from her bed to check on its progress. In her determination for growth, she overwaters it, causing dirt water to overflow onto the carpet. Then, to dry out the dirt again, she sits the cup on the front porch for sunlight. I can see that she is

---

[18] Ann Voskamp, *WayMaker: Finding the Way to the Life You've Always Dreamed Of* (Nashville: Thomas Nelson, 2022), 30.

losing patience. I assure her that though it looks like nothing is growing, underneath, in the dark, the seed is growing. "You'll see it one day," I tell her.

But I'm not that convinced in my own life. Season after season, all I see is dirt. In desperation to not feel pain, I over-water and dry out the promised seed. Faith looks like doing everything I can for the seed to grow. But, in reality, faith is putting down the water pail and allowing things to germinate, believing God is working even if the seed looks dormant. It's trusting that He's working in the darkness. Looking at our dirt through God's lens, we see He's got His Holy pitcher of Living Water ready. Hope means to trust in God's goodness even when it seems nothing is growing.

My oldest son's name, Douglas, is also his father's, and my husband's deceased father's: Douglas Michael Turner. So technically, he's Douglas Michael Turner the third. We all call him Douglas, while his friends call him Doug. I knew he had a special calling on his life from early on. Over the years, as I pray for him, the Holy Spirit often overwhelms me to the point of tears. Each time, God brings to remembrance the unique calling on Douglas's life, and still, to this day, I feel the need to continue to remind him of it.

Douglas has a strong will. He made his entrance into the world with nearly twenty-four hours of intense labor and then refused to breastfeed, but eventually, he got it. He relentlessly climbed out of his crib at eighteen months, refusing to sleep in it anymore, so he peacefully slept in a twin bed at not even two years old. Every chore assigned to him became a battle he was determined to win. We engaged in countless arguments over music selections and electronics, and those disagreements left us both with hurt feelings. He possesses this knack for persisting until he eventually gets his way.

His thirst for knowledge is admirable. As early as age two, he sat with me for hours as I read him book after book. He soaked in every bit of knowledge, and by age four, he was reading. Unfortunately, the half-day kindergarten where they learned their letters didn't cut it, so I began homeschooling him. His love for literature extended into middle school. As a result, he's a whole grade level ahead of his peers when he finally starts private school in eighth grade. In the summers, he spent most of his time in the backyard reading. His curiosity for learning never stopped, and his grades always reflected that. A few weeks after his seventeenth birthday, he graduated with honors.

We've always shared a special bond. I remember him lying on my chest for the first time, looking into those big brown eyes, feeling a deep love. There's something about a mother and her firstborn son you can't explain. I recall dropping him off at preschool the first day, sobbing because I hated to leave him, and as the parents were all leaving, a dad turned to me and said, "It's only three hours." My love for this child, who's now a man, continues to be fierce.

Filling the oldest role in a family of five is a challenge. Under leadership qualities on applications, Douglas often wrote, "oldest of five." Having four people looking up to you for guidance is a lofty position. He has taken this role seriously for a considerable amount of years. With only twenty-two months between him and his younger sister, he felt the need to look after her. More times than we can count, people mistake them as twins. Their bond is certainly similar. Abby adored him and cherished every moment with her older brother. All the siblings did.

He confessed Jesus was the Lord of his life at an early age. One night, seeing how exhausted I was as I tucked him into bed, he laid his hands on me and prayed the sweetest prayer for strength. His sensitivity to God and others is something I admire. I will forever have a picture of him as a small child with tears running down his face at the altar of our church, crying out to God for a renewed heart.

He has a gift for memorization. He memorized verse after verse in his Awana program. Still, to this day, he can recite the verses he learned at an early age. However, he constantly struggled to view himself as an intelligent, creative, sound-minded young man through God's eyes. For far too long, he sold himself short.

After our family relocated to Mississippi, he found it challenging to adapt. I'm sure it was because he thrived in the church environment during our time in Alabama, which showcased his singing, dancing, and acting talents over four years. In hindsight, I can see that he truly excelled in those moments. His creativity blossomed because he has a genuine passion for being on stage. In middle school, he had an unconventional fashion sense. For several years, he proudly sported a fedora hat, symbolizing his unique style and creative spirit.

When we moved to Mississippi, I knew I needed to find a creative outlet for him, but I struggled to find anything in our rural area. Trying hard to fit into our sports-minded community, he joined the school soccer team. While I think he loved soccer, he still struggled to fit in and longed for a creative outlet. Being almost two years younger than his classmates didn't help. Over time, I saw his enthusiasm for life fade.

Darkness remains over him for several years as he cannot fight the lies of unworthiness. First, it is drinking—just socially at first. Then, it leads to sneaking out with friends late at night. Then, finally, the house fire breaks the dam. Even though we promise our kids that we'll make it through as a family, we all see a severe shift in Douglas.

As each day rolls into the next, he becomes angrier and angrier. Carrying more pain than we realize from the fire, grasping to fit in with friends, and COVID screwing up his junior year, he begins to spiral. His drinking becomes a problem. Friends drop him off at the house several times, so drunk he barely knows his name, causing Mike to stay up with him all night.

I smell something strange one day, getting out of the car at the house. Rounding the bend to the backside of the shed, I catch him smoking weed. Grasping for straws, we engage him in counseling. After graduating high school, his frequent sneaking out increased to nearly every night. Most nights, he didn't come home till the morning, if at all. Douglas goes to church, sits at the dinner table, and tries to hold it all together, but we argue more than we get along. He slips into deeper darkness each day. Dabbling in drugs becomes full-blown abuse. We are all scared. I'm not sure any of us grasp the torment he feels inside. Just like me, his numbing and coping mechanisms get out of control.

Everyone in our family is hurting, and I try to love all the children and Mike well. Every chance I get, I speak God's love over them. However, in the months of Douglas' spiral, things get even worse. Abby's anxiety skyrockets, and Elijah has a heart defect that needs my attention. It is my very own private nightmare.

Being the primary caretaker of a family is a juggling act. Most days, I run from one appointment to the next, unsure what to do or which way to go, trying to keep all the plates spinning and avoid any from crashing down. Exhaustion overtakes me with the days filled with Douglas and Abby's counseling appointments and Elijah's cardiology appointments.

I did everything I knew to hold it together, but how do you silence lies that you aren't a good enough mom? I hide in shame my son's drug use from his siblings and our friends. It seems there is drama and crisis around every corner, not to mention the endless paperwork from the fire and the effort to build a new house. It is all too much.

Stress tears at our marriage as we feel the weight of it all.

Douglas's world teeters. More substance abuse. Almost every night out. Scary fighting. We take away his car. We hold his phone from him. We ground him, talk to him, and beg him to stop. Nothing helps.

One night, around 2 a.m., I woke in a panic, feeling this urge to find Douglas even though he hadn't been home for several nights. Shaking Mike awake, I beg him to get Douglas. Something in my spirit tells me he isn't okay. Guessing where he might be, Mike drives thirty minutes to the next town to his friend's house. After repeatedly calling his phone and praying God would help us locate him. Finally, incredibly high, he stumbles to the car from some unknown apartment.

The Holy Spirit's nudging saved my son's life. I later found out he planned to kill himself that night. Always and forever trust and obey the still, small voice of the Holy Spirit.

God gently reminds me even now that when life seems out of control, God is still in control. Isaiah 29:22 says, *"Thus says the Lord…and they shall bring your sons in their arms, and your daughters shall be carried on their shoulders."*

This verse refers to the Israelites being carried back from their physical captivity to Babylon, and it's just how Jesus tenderly carries us through our time of need. I once read that sheep lie down and wait for the shepherd to carry them on his shoulder when hurt or physically weak.[19]

The same is true of the Lord, *our* Shepherd. He's not only pursuing us in our time of need—He's carrying us.

Never for one moment does God require us to crawl out of the valley to climb up the mountain to reach Him. Instead, he finds us in the valley and pursues us there, bringing comfort in our most profound, darkest moments. Never once does he leave us alone.

Even if no growth sprouts through the dirt, God's still working in the dark where no one sees.

In all my best efforts, I attempt to ease my son's hurt if only I could find him the right help, medication, or an outstanding mentor. I think that if only he could grasp how much I long to see him set free from his suffering, he'll walk away from all the addiction. Something has to give. Finally, in a desperate attempt to save his life, I google drug rehabs and begin to make calls.

Two days later, my son and I stand in his room, packing.

The more we pack, the angrier he grows. At first, he agrees to go to rehab, but then reality sets in. Lying on the bed, refusing to pack, fiddling with one of his necklaces, he says, "I don't think I need to go."

Is he for real?

As I read through the packing list the rehab center sent us, my blood began to boil. Can't he see I'm trying to help?

Holding back tears, I tell him, "Please help me help you."

Instead, my now grown-up baby boy begins screaming that the only way to get him to rehab is to call the police. Desperate to calm him down, I cup his face, looking him straight in the eye, and speak purpose and identity over him: "You were made for greatness. God has a mighty plan for your life filled with purpose, but you have to be healthy to accomplish it. Do you hear me? You must get well."

---

[19] W. Phillip Keller, *A Shepherd Looks at Psalm 23* (Grand Rapids: Zondervan, 2007).

Nodding his head in agreement, he begins to cry as he finishes packing his clothes. For one moment, a sliver of light pierces through the darkness that entangles his mind. At the heart of any addiction is the need to feel loved and needed.

I drive Douglas five hours the next day to rehab, believing with my entire being this would be the place he'd find help. As we go, I thank God he revealed Douglas's struggle early on, and hopefully, this is just a blip on his road to success. In a few short months, he'll be going off to college.

His hand reaches for mine as we walk up the center's driveway. With liquid grief streaming down my face, I don't pull my hand away. Instead, I turn toward him, telling him he'll be home soon, healed and whole, ready to start college in the fall. He nods. My heart breaks, yet I'm hopeful. I can still remember driving home with an unexplainable peace for the future.

The four months of Douglas being gone are a blur. Exhaustion is an understatement of how we feel driving the five hours back and forth to visit him. Sometimes, we go with the kids; sometimes, Mike and I go alone.

Additionally, there are phone calls and hours spent in family counseling, unsure how much progress he's making—all the while trying to maintain life at home with the other four children without outside help because you just don't tell your friends that your son is in a drug rehab program. The ache within my body and the fog in my brain is the same as when I cared for my sick dad those eight long months before he died. Caring for a sick loved one makes you bone tired. I try to hold it all together, but the weariness weighs on me.

Douglas returns home for three months before relapsing on Christmas Eve on a family trip, which ends in an angry outburst upsetting the other children. On New Year's Eve, Mike drives him to another rehab only an hour and a half from the house. Bit by bit, our family faces the reality that Douglas has a full-blown addiction problem. I avoid it for the first few months, thinking it's just a phase. The truth is we all struggle differently. Each person is unique in the way trauma reacts within them. Some people quickly move on after a house fire, and others do not.

Reality seeps in, crushing my hope. We try to hold everything together on the outside while disappointment and shame eat away on the inside.

There are unexpected moments of grief, each different than the other. First, my father's death, then my mom's unexpected cancer diagnosis, then the house fire, then Elijah's heart surgery, and finally now my son's addiction. Everything is causing grief to bubble to the surface, demanding attention. Each season of grief is similar but with different intensities.

I remember cleaning my son's room a few days after he left again for rehab, crying. The reality of his addiction comes flooding in. My heart aches from missing him terribly and wondering if I've done everything I could for him. I thought I could love him to wholeness. I tried to be with him every time he reached out. Addiction feels like the most brutal hit of them all. How can I fill the emptiness? How can I love him through this when nothing I do seems to be enough? Isn't a mother supposed to protect her children from something like this happening?

When I feel like I've failed at the very thing God created me to do, the intensity of grief is almost unbearable. Yet again, my heart can't grasp this new type of pain. I sit wondering what has gone wrong. How on earth can this be my reality? Do I trust God to make everything right–whatever that means? I didn't know what to do with my unmet dreams and prayers for him and our family.

Later, I read this quote: "One of the hardest things you will ever have to do, my dear, is to grieve the loss of a person who is still alive."[20]

Life is now full of trips to rehab, family and individual counseling sessions, and phone call after phone call with people on Douglas's team, all trying to move him in the right direction. The goal was to transition him back to living at home.

One of the best things about this rehab facility is meeting with other parents who also have a child struggling with addiction. There's

---

[20] Jeannette Walls, *The Glass Castle: A Memoir* (United Kingdom: Pocket Books, 2007).

a comfort in surrounding ourselves with others dealing with the same type of suffering. Together, we all sit in a room, and for one hour, we feel understood. For one hour, we share the trauma of our lives. Circling the room, we each speak our story shame-free. We celebrate the wins and losses, meeting each other with kindness. It's here where my husband and I find the endurance and steadfastness to continue moving forward.

Every other Sunday, our sons join us in the common area in the main house at the rehab. Each person shares. Our family's turn comes, and Douglas starts by saying he's had a pretty good week and is thankful to have parents who support him. I go next, sharing how grateful I am for this place. Mike speaks of his need for God's love to love others well. Our vulnerability, met with sacred understanding, comforts our weary souls.

Is this what it looks like to embrace reality? Hearts sincere and vulnerable, busting through the shame by speaking out with others on similar journeys. We find healing when we show up for ourselves and others with compassion.

One particular day, another mom shared that she struggles to trust God. She questions, "Will her son always have a substance use disorder?" Not many of us can openly admit that we don't trust God. It is deceptively easy to think we trust God until life doesn't go as planned.

I think often about that mother's words the following week. It's strange how we pretend, especially to ourselves, that we live in surrender to God. We forge our path, trying ever so slightly to manipulate everything our way. It's easy to do… until you can't.

I have "done everything right" to raise Douglas to be a man of God, yet it isn't enough. I never thought his life would take such a drastic turn—not in a million, trillion years. Life isn't how I imagine it for him. I grieve the loss of what I expect life to look like for him; all the unfulfilled expectations seem endless. I long to tie a bow around the story and feel a sense of closure, but the closure I desperately long for never comes.

In the book of John, Jesus receives word from Martha and Mary that their brother Lazarus is ill.

Shortly before this, Mary wiped Jesus's feet with her hair while Martha busily prepared dinner. Now, here they are, overtaken with fear, calling for Jesus because they know he'll be able to heal their brother quickly. But surprisingly, because Jesus loves them, He waits two days before making the trip to Lazarus.

Wait—what? Because He loves them, he waits? Who waits because they love someone? Shouldn't it be the opposite, going as quickly as possible out of love?

Two days of waiting and then two days of travel equal four days of Lazarus being in the tomb by the time Jesus arrives.

True to her personality, Mary runs to Him at the first sight of Jesus, lamenting that if only He'd come right away, her brother would still be alive. Martha stays in the house. Sometimes, I feel like Mary, filled with grief, crying out to Jesus, hanging on to the last bit of hope. I ask, "Why did you let all of this happen? Jesus, why didn't you intervene?"

Sometimes, I feel like Martha sitting in the house, grieving without any hope. Why bother to run out to Jesus at all? There's no hope for Lazarus. Hope was dead.

Jesus told Mary, *"Your brother will rise again." Martha responded, 'I know he will rise again in the resurrection on the last day"* (John 11:24).

Jesus replied, *"I am the resurrection and the life. Whoever believes in me though he die, yet shall he live, and everyone who lives and believes in me will never die. Do you believe this?' She said to him. 'Yes, Lord' I believed that you are the Christ, the Son of God, who is coming into the world"* (John 11:17-27).

Wrestling with our faith draws us closer to Jesus. Meditating that Jesus took four days to respond may only be an incubator for bitterness to grow. Questioning brought to the feet of Jesus opens our hearts to greater intimacy. You can rattle the offense from your heart by asking Him all your questions.

The three siblings, Mary, Martha, and Lazarus, had lost their parents. That means that with Lazarus dead, the two sisters stand alone in a culture predominantly run by men. Lazarus is not only their brother; he is their security, livelihood, and possibly even their only source of income. This loss strikes at Martha's core fear of being alone. She fears the future because of the unknown. Who will provide for them, and what if she and her sister aren't okay without Lazarus?

Jesus, fully knowing her fears and concerns, asks a different question: "I am the resurrection and life… Do you believe this?"

Jesus doesn't ask Martha to believe in a miracle. He doesn't even ask if she thinks He can raise Lazarus from the dead. Instead, He asks if she believes in who He says He is, regardless of her circumstances. His question cuts to the heart of her fear of the future.

In other words, Jesus is saying, "Martha, after all the history we've shared and all you've seen over the past two years, do you believe I am the resurrection and the life?"

With a grief-stricken heart, Martha looks at the only person who could save her brother and says, "Yes, Lord. Even now, I believe."

Jesus shows us that it takes even greater faith to believe God is who He says He is when the miracle doesn't come.

Days after my dad's cancer diagnosis, I sat with a friend, fearing the same thing Martha did. Is everything going to be okay? The future is so unknown. My friend turns toward me and says, "God will work it out. It could be worse."

Will He?

*Yes, it could be worse, but at this time, it is my worst.*

In an instant, my feelings are swept up under the rug, no longer validated.

Now, let's read the next part of the story of Lazarus:

*"Jesus wept."*

I have read these two words before. I've even heard sermons preached on how Jesus feels and experiences human emotions. Now, however, I see these two words in a different light. Never before have I noticed Jesus; God himself feels the reality of the situation. He allows the grief and sadness to move through Him for a moment. Jesus chose to feel the reality of Lazarus's death, validating and comforting Mary and Martha.

Jesus grieves with the sisters, affirming their pain. With tears running down His face, He says to humanity, "I ache with you, and you'll never walk this journey of grief alone."

As Christians, we often bypass the crucifixion to enjoy the resurrection. But can we have the resurrection without the crucifixion? We lose the beauty and wonder of the resurrection if we move away from the crucifixion too quickly. Jesus chose to walk into suffering, revealing that we can't have a resolution without suffering.

Paul writes some startling words in the book of Philippians we'd rather skip over: *"I want to know Christ—yes, to know the power of His resurrection and participation in His sufferings, becoming like Him in His death, and so, somehow, attaining to the resurrection from the dead"* (Philippians 3:10-11).

Part of the journey through the valley of grief is facing the reality of the trauma. There is no sugarcoating it. Yes, it's as bad as you think. But His presence is with us.

Today, like Martha, we declare, "Yes, I believe in the resurrection of Jesus," while also weeping at the reality of our situation.

Maybe, just maybe, it's about holding the tension between the two realities: grieving for what's lost while hoping for the future—because where Jesus is, there's always hope.

The last few years, I've felt like Martha stuck between the crucifixion and the resurrection, between what was and what would one day be.

One thing remains constant: His Presence.

He is with us, behind us, and before us. God's there, reminding us our story isn't over yet.

Mary and Martha's story isn't over. And neither is ours. Jesus turns the page to their story by telling the sisters to remove the stone from

Lazarus's tomb. Martha protests, saying, "It will stink. Don't you know it's been four days?"

Is this how we stop Jesus, too? We've seen him perform miracles for other people. We even believe he can turn our weeping into joy. However, the suffering has lasted longer than expected. We've stormed heaven with no answers. All hope feels lost. And we don't want to deal with the stink of ripping off the bandage.

We know Jesus can transform our pain, but… won't it stink? We've neatly folded the grave clothes of our unmet dreams and prayers and placed them in the back of the tomb, never to drag them back out again. So what's the use anymore?

Jesus can make all things new, but revisiting the hurt and the pain of trauma just doesn't seem worth it.

If we are honest with the reality of our situation, won't the smell of it waft out? Then, everyone will know I lack the faith to believe. I couldn't possibly tell anyone about Douglas's drug problem. The stench of our reality would scare people off, or maybe they would think less of us.

I fear the stink.

If we're ever going to see the restoration, we need to realize it will be messy before it gets better. Trusting Jesus to roll away the stone allows Him to unwind the grave clothes of bitterness, resentment, denial, and disappointment and open our eyes to the brightness of the future. He is the resurrection and the life.

Do we believe this?

*"Then Jesus said, "Did I not tell you that if you believe, you will see the glory of God?"* (John 11:40).

Dear friend, one day, we will *all* see the glory of God in our situation!

I continued to read John 11:43, where Jesus shouted, *"Lazarus, come out!"*

I reread it repeatedly, envisioning Jesus shouting, "Douglas, come out of that grave!" He's calling my son by his name. He wants him out of the darkness as much, if not more, than I do. So I further read, *"The dead man came out"* (Luke 11:44). I underlined it. Douglas was the only one who could walk out of his grave. I couldn't do it for him, and neither could God. Douglas had to take the steps out of the grave.

So, as desperately I wanted him fixed, I surrendered him to God. Not that day, but eventually, an unexplainable peace settled upon me. Douglas would soon be eighteen—not a baby anymore, but a man. It wasn't my job to save him, and as much as that hurt, I had to face that reality. My job was simply to love him.

Do you know what the best part of John 11 is?

*"The dead man came out, his hands and feet wrapped with strips of linen and a cloth around his face. Jesus said to them, 'Take off the grave clothes and let him go'* (John 11:44).

Here's the reality: when nothing seems to be emerging from the dirt, and the stone's been in place for more days than you can count, it's easy for your heart to be torn and start losing hope. Hope will begin to leak out when the world starts crashing in, causing you to believe that things will never change and there's no hope for the days ahead.

Jesus stands in front of your tomb, calling. When something or someone emerges from the grave, others help unwind the grave clothes. We're built for community, so we don't have to do it alone. None of us do. God calls us to help each other unwind the mess of the darkness.

## DIGGING DEEPER:

1. Have you ever had to grieve the loss of a person still alive? How did you navigate through the complexities of such a situation?

2. When faced with unimaginable circumstances, how do you find the faith and trust to surrender your pain and unmet dreams to God?

# CHAPTER 6

## WHERE ARE YOU, GOD?

> *"God is often silent when we prefer that he speak, and he interrupts us when we prefer that he stay silent. His ways are not our ways."*[21]

All of us carry suffering differently. But for many, suffering can be likened to walking through life with a brown paper bag on our heads, searching for a way out and wondering if we've done something wrong to deserve this harsh treatment. Questions arise about whether we are living life correctly and if maybe we've failed along the way. In our darkest moments, we're uncertain when or if God will intervene to make things right.

When I strip away the layers of my grief, I grieve the loss of what I thought life should look like—grieving the change in plans because this isn't what I expected. Compared to the "perfectly normal" lives around me, I feel inadequate, like I don't measure up because here I am still suffering. Is it my responsibility to make everything right as if I can somehow heal my brokenness? Then, there's still that gnawing feeling that God has abandoned me.

The heartbreaking turn of events with Douglas breaks something

---

[21] M. Craig Barnes, *When God Interrupts* (Downer's Grove, IL: InterVarsity Press, 1996), 135.

within me, making this truth a reality: "You're blessed when you're at the end of your rope. With less of you, there is more of God and his rule."[22] Suffering does lead to more of God in our lives. I want to shrink back and pretend it isn't all happening because living a life surrendered to the suffering feels too much, too vulnerable, and too painful.

Where is more of God?

It's in His Word: *We are blessed when we're at the end of our rope,* "but why don't I feel so blessed? Wouldn't I feel more blessed if God, in His sovereignty, reached down and healed my family?

This question weighs heavier as the days tick on. Another fight with my teenager left me busted and bruised. All the words from our argument race through my mind: "You're never there for me," yells this angry teen, "Why can't our family be normal?"

Trust me. I want it to be normal, too. If only we could be more patient and loving and act like we have it all together. I desperately want God to zap us with all the wisdom and make it easier for all of us.

Is there no other way forward than through the valley? Isn't it time for my miracle? I have given my entire life to Christ. Can't God see how hard I'm trying? Don't I deserve the "more of God?"

I escape behind the bathroom door with the water running loud enough so no one can hear my groans and howls of surrendering to the brokenness. The bathroom floor becomes my altar—because who wants to listen to a wailing woman Sunday after Sunday? My children are embarrassed enough by my uncontrollable tears. I cry more than ever this season, often escaping to the bathroom, hoping no one will see or hear the liquid grief.

What if the only way to surrender is to grieve the unexpected? And the harsh reality is the only way to grieve the unexpected is to trust God's got something else in the works. I knew I needed to trust Him. —it's a

---

[22] Matthew 5:3 MSG

whole new kind of surrender when it seems there's no earthly way it will all work out.

When we see no way to turn around our reality, we don't typically trust more. We pull ourselves together on the outside while self-destructing on the inside—those lies that God is only there for those who have it all together rattle around so loud we've convinced ourselves if only we tried harder, God would show up and show off.

Popular Christian culture says that we have to be more for God to get more of God. Read more. Give more. Serve more. Be more.

I know it all too well. There are days when the sharp edges of grief cut so deep that I grasp to remember that God never leaves. Of course, I know this in my mind, but I struggle to see God's hand working and question it in my heart. Maybe He forgot me.

Worried and worn out, I lie on the bathroom floor crying, questions rushing through my head: *How can loving God make you feel so raw and vulnerable?*

Douglas and I have come so far, yet here we are again and again, bruised and beaten by arguing. Haven't I done the work to become whole? Why does my anger keep flaring? "God," I pray, "please reach down and fix all this. Show me your glory. Fix this reality of mine."

I fight the lies with the Truth to get myself out of that bathroom: "Don't despise your pain because it's a highway to an encounter with Jesus," I tell myself. I am desperate to hear from God. So I pull out the Word:

*"Immediately, he made the disciples get into the boat and go before him to the other side, to Bethsaida, while he dismissed the crowd...And when evening came, the boat was out on the sea, and he was alone on the land. And he saw they were making headway painfully, for the wind was against them. And about the fourth watch of the night, he came to them, walking on the sea. He meant to pass by them, but when they saw him walking on the sea, they thought it was a ghost and cried out, for they saw him and were terrified. But immediately, he spoke to them and said, 'Take heart; it is I. Do not be afraid.' And he got into the boat with them, and the wind ceased. And they were utterly astounded...."* (Mark 6:45-51).

As the disciples fight the storm, I wonder if they question Jesus's whereabouts. They followed Jesus, trying their best to learn from Him, and He sent them straight into a storm! Confusion must fall upon them as they fiercely fight against the wind and the waves.

Questions must be swirling around, such as, "What is going on? Why are we being punished with a storm when we were helping others with Jesus? Where is He? Why is this happening?"

I don't think the disciples imagine climbing into a boat one afternoon, pushing it into the Sea of Galilee, and not smoothly making it to the other side. On land, Jesus communes with His Father into the evening and long into the night. As a result, Jesus *saw [from land] they were making headway painfully, for the wind was against them"* (Mark 6:48). In Matthew's version, it says, *"The ship was…tossed with waves"* (Matthew 14:24).

Exhausted from rowing for hours and fighting for their lives, the disciples desperately cry out for help, only to be met with silence. Unbeknownst to them, Jesus stands on the shore, watching from afar. With each row of their oars, darkness sucks them further in, possibly making them question everything they believe: "Where's Jesus? He doesn't care. Have we done something to deserve this storm? He can perform all those miracles for others but leaves us stranded in a storm!"

Why does Jesus wait so long to make His presence known?

The thing is, He is there all along.

*"About the fourth watch of the night, He comes to them walking on the sea"* (Mark 6:48). The fourth watch is from three in the morning until sunrise. That's a long time to be fighting a storm! They would have preferred Jesus to show up a little earlier. Don't we all?

I often feel like the disciples, straining, fighting wave after wave, becoming increasingly exhausted from the storm, and wrestling with no answers. The grief from all the unexpected trauma is too much to bear. I feel forgotten. And Jesus is looking on, waiting from the shore to make His presence known. It feels like a mockery for Jesus to appear in the fourth watch. Why didn't He show up earlier?

When Jesus walks on water, it says, *"[He] meant to pass them by."* The frightened disciples thought He was a ghost. (Mark 6:48)

Why would Jesus pass them by in their time of need? It seems outside Jesus's character. Even as I write, it seems ridiculous—but isn't that what we do, too? We accuse God of walking by in our darkest moments, or we even accuse Him of not showing up. Night after night, we cry out, wondering why He has abandoned us in our time of need.

But here's the thing: If we haven't developed the habit of being fully aware of His presence, would we even realize He was trying to make His presence known to us?

Could it be that God is trying to show up in unexpected new ways, and I'm unaware it's Him?

"The phrase 'pass by them' does not mean that Jesus passed by to ignore His disciples. The phrase is also used in the Old Testament when God "passed by" Moses, revealing Himself to him. So, Jesus' appearance reassured the disciples that He had sent them out on the water and would see them through their troubles."[23]

In 1 Kings 19, God converses with Elijah and "passes by him" in verse 11. God doesn't pass by Elijah to ignore him. Instead, God passes by to show Elijah His glory and to extend comfort, strength, and courage to Elijah in the form of a gentle whisper.

Jesus didn't abandon the disciples. Instead, he revealed more of himself to them. Until now, the disciples didn't know Jesus as the God who walked on water! Then, in the fourth hour, when they least expected, He reveals a part of His character in a way they had never experienced!

In the middle of our dark storms, we wonder where Jesus is, unaware that He patiently awaits from the shoreline, longing to reveal something new. Who could've imagined our storms inviting us to experience more of God?

These passages help me see a new pattern in God's Word. Genesis 21 reveals the same invitation to Hagar. After wandering in the wilderness

---

[23] Rodney L Cooper, *Holman New Testament Commentary* (Nashville: Broadman & Holman Publishers, 2000)..

of Beer-sheba with her son, Ishmael, Hagar was desperate without water when *"she put the child under one of the bushes. Then she sat down opposite him a good way off, about the distance of a bowshot, then she said, 'Let me not look on the death of the child,' As she sat opposite him, she lifted her voice and wept. And God heard the boy, and the angel of God called to Hagar from heaven and said to her, 'What troubles you, Hagar? Fear not, for God has heard the voice of the boy where he is.' So, God opened her eyes, and she saw a well of water"* (Genesis 21: 15-19).

There are days when our vision is cloudy from weeping, and we think, "What's the point? God doesn't even hear my prayers!" In these moments, remember that it only takes a single drop of water from heaven to quench our thirsty souls.

The next time you wonder where God is, remember He's trying to show us the previously undiscovered, life-giving waters of a nearby well. Since the Word of God is living and active, isn't this true for us today? If God walked on water to the disciples, He is also stepping out to us in the middle of our storm.

Waiting and longing through the fourth watch allows us to encounter God in new ways. It's where we experience *more of God*.

Take comfort. Life is waves. Grief comes in waves. Suffering can even come in waves. But God's presence doesn't come in waves. It is forever present, never absent. He's not passing us by in our time of need. He is Lord over the storms and with us in the storms! He hears our cries. God provides us the comfort, strength, and courage to endure daily.

Life is not linear. Doing good and following the rules doesn't equal a life without suffering. God isn't giving us a grade on how well we are doing in life and deeming us to suffer when we mess up. Instead, He looks at my heart and how yielded I am to His love. One thing I know for sure:

The hard-core reality is that we can do everything right and still land in difficult places. We cannot save ourselves from suffering, and we certainly can't protect our families from it. We are broken people in a broken world. *Our* job is to offer ourselves to God and allow Him to use us. We see His glory most through suffering rather than Him reaching down and plucking us out of misery through a miracle.

Frequently, we overlook our minor role in a larger plan. It's easy to lose sight of the fact that we are not the main characters in our story; God is. Despite our suffering, God has chosen us for this role.

The kids and I read about a woman who became a missionary in India. At an early age, she feels the call to serve the nation, except she has a debilitating battle with neuralgia that causes excruciating pain. Amy Carmichael had many reasons to refuse the call to become a missionary. Being sent home time after time because of her illness, I'm sure she considered throwing in the towel. Amy's outlook on suffering differed from most. She wrote, "Let us not be surprised when we have to face difficulties. When the wind blows hard on a tree, the roots stretch and grow stronger. Let it be so with us. Let us not be weaklings, yielding to every wind that blows, but strong in spirit to resist."[24]

Amy ran through the darkness, allowing the light of Christ to guide her instead of giving up. No sickness, pit of depression, or loneliness stopped her from accomplishing the work of the Lord. She stood on the promise that no storm could outdo the light of Christ. She lived life knowing that Jesus was the One who calmed her storms.[25]

In the face of suffering, Amy stopped asking, "Where are you, God?" and instead asked, 'Where are You working even in my suffering?"

When Amy finally landed in India, she became one of the world's most well-known human trafficking activists. Serving for fifty-three years, she saved hundreds of girls, most of whom called her "mother." Amy stepped into her suffering, refusing for it to define her. She once wrote, "It is so fatally easy to forget that we are not here to enjoy life, to live pleasantly, without stabs and rending griefs that leave scars…[but] 'that I may know Him, and…the fellowship of His sufferings'" (Phil. 3:10).[26]

---

[24] Pamela Rose Williams, "21 Top Amy Carmichael Quotes," What Christians Want To Know, accessed April 1, 2024, https://www.whatchristianswanttoknow.com/21-top-amy-carmichael-quotes.
[25] Janet Benge and Geoff Benge, Amy Carmichael: Rescuer of Precious Gems (Seattle, WA: YWAM Pub., 1998).
[26] Leslie Ludy, "Amy Carmichael: Her Legacy of Faith & How It Changed My Life," Set

Trusting God kept Amy moving forward through the darkness. It isn't easy to surrender to the fellowship of His sufferings. The pain and the hurt are real, and it can seem that nothing makes a lick of sense. Life, as you know, is flipped upside down. You feel like you're moving through quicksand, longing for God to pluck you out of this suffering. With grief, it's easy to believe life will always be this way. It won't. All of the hurt and pain will lessen, and grief will become a part of you.

Amy kept pressing forward. Then, after spending many years serving on behalf of helpless children, she fell and broke her back, leaving her crippled and confined to her bedroom for two decades. Finally, after grieving life as she knew it, she began asking God where He was in the middle of her suffering. She chose not to let her situation separate her from God and started writing books. Grief didn't stop her. Amy's thirteen books in the last twenty years of her life encourage many even today.

Plucking her out of her suffering wasn't an option God gave her.

When faced with significant loss, no matter what it is, there's a time to move forward, knowing that we're not alone. Each step requires us to embrace our feelings and then, in return, pour them out to God, believing He is making all things right.

Acknowledging He hasn't forgotten us and still speaks and moves today is part of the process. As you embrace these invitations for more of Him, you'll be amazed at how He speaks through suffering, revealing things you've never seen before.

A few days after the house fire, my husband sits comforting Abby as she pours her heart out. She admits feeling abandoned by God. She asks, "Why didn't God prevent the fire? Why did I have to be alone here with the other kids?"

Mike can see it in her eyes; she feels abandoned by all of us.

Softly, he tells her to close her eyes and envision herself lying on the

---

Apart, accessed April 1, 2024, https://setapart.org/amy-carmichael/.

couch in the living room the day of the fire when she first saw the flames. Then, he asks her a question we often asked in a prayer ministry we were a part of several years ago: "Where is Jesus?"

It takes her a minute or two, but she closes her eyes and says, "I see him outside the window where the flames bellow out from the attic. He's outside holding back the flames."

Moving through each scene of that day, Mike asks her, "Where is Jesus?" Abby never says, "He's not there" or "I can't find Him." Instead, she sees Him holding back flames or comforting her and her siblings.

"How about when Brandon's running down the hall toward the door, and the windows were breaking?" Mike asked.

"Dad, I see Jesus running with him, preventing the glass from hurting him and holding the smoke back," Abby responds.

Tears flow, and praises rise. He never leaves us! Although it looks like those four kids walked out of the smoke-filled house alone, there is another in the fire! God never left them!

At age fifteen, Abby knows God as her rescuer. He's always at work, even when He seems silent.

Be patient and observant to see the working hand of God.

Resist the urge to bypass emotions. It can take some time. While others stop in the darkness, we can pause and ask, "Where is Jesus?"

Healing comes in the pause.

The healing comes in the moments of silence, where we acknowledge the grief and pain. "The notes I handle no better than many pianists. But the pauses between the notes—ah, that is where the art resides".[27] Like the pause in the music, it's not a void but an opportunity to recognize our feelings and ask, "Jesus, where are you now?"

---

[27] Artur Schnabel (1882-1951), Austrian pianist and composer.

Jesus remains ever-present, regardless of our exhaustion, fear, or overwhelming grief. He is there when we need Him, and there is more of Him than we can feel or imagine. Sometimes, it takes being at the end of ourselves to see God face to face. There is a reason the verse says, *"We are blessed when we are at the end of our rope."*[28] He meets us at the end of our rope, where He does His best work.

Grief is not the opposite of hope! On the contrary, grief is a sign of hope because God shows up unexpectedly. Waves may persist, but we must believe He is always looking and waiting to come to us, walking on water.

God's expanding my imagination of His ways. In my mind, all I could see was suffering. I thought there was no way through except to grin and bear it. Endless waves of pain and despair attempt to take over. Hopelessness arises when *we* see no end or purpose to the suffering. But where God is, there is always Hope! When it feels as if all hope is lost, close your eyes and ask, "Where are you, Jesus?" Hope diminishes when we envision a future without Jesus. Know where Jesus is, and you feel the waves of peace.

Days later, I sat outside in the early morning, attempting to catch a few moments with God before the kids woke up. Even though God has revealed Himself to me in the past week, I feel the sadness creeping in. Instead of pushing it away, I allow the sadness to sit with me momentarily. Pausing. Inhaling and exhaling, I close my eyes and say, "Jesus, where are you now?"

I saw a beautiful vision of Jesus taking my hand and leading me to an open space, and we began to dance. He looks passionately into my tear-filled eyes as a wave of peace washes over me. There it is, sweet surrender. Through this intimate relationship, I am able to surrender to His ways beyond my comprehension.

We lose our way, getting tangled up, wanting God to remove the pain. Feelings and emotions inform us, but God's Presence leads us through the valley. Focusing on the miracle rather than on God's Presence only further isolates us from God in our grieving.

---

[28] Matthew 5:3 MSG

I've spent countless nights wondering where God was and why He wasn't performing a miracle to end my suffering. Slowly, I've learned there's unimaginable peace in letting go of the constant fight to understand why this is happening and releasing the need to find meaning. It is not about not caring, escaping your reality, or leaving behind the person you've lost. Instead, it's about trusting God in the grieving and lamenting. It's all about surrendering.

One day, as I wash dishes, I hear the Holy Spirit say, "That's enough! No more rehab. No more prayers for Douglas's healing. Just worship and praise me even though you don't see the miracle. Even in the suffering." Ultimately, it's not how we grieve that distances us from God; it's where we put our trust. I placed more trust in the miracle of suffering vanishing than in relying on God's presence to sustain me. That doesn't mean I should stop praying or believing. Instead, I have to trust the mystery of God's ways. I have to trust Him.

I don't have all the answers, nor do I know why God allows some to suffer more than others. But I have learned this: the only way to make sense of it all is to pursue Him as He relentlessly pursues us. We seek Him by surrendering it all, even the problematic unanswered prayers. I've found that when you give Him all the questioning and trust Him in the journey, He will provide you with peace to continue, and you will experience His presence like never before.

As we wrestle, let's not forget, "For everything comes from him and exists by his power and is intended for his glory. All glory to him forever! Amen" (Romans 11:36). Paul states, "But if we are to share His glory, we must also share His suffering" (Romans 8:17).

Whether we feel His presence or not, we continue to pray till the very end: *"But even if he does not, we want you to know, Your Majesty, that we will not serve your gods or worship the image of gold you have set up"* (Daniel 3:18). God is still good and worthy of praise no matter what!

## DIGGING DEEPER:

1. Have you ever experienced a moment where you felt the sadness creeping in, and instead of pushing it away, you allowed it to sit with you? How did that affect your connection with God?

2. What would your future look like without God in it? Take a moment to imagine the future without God in it. Journal what you felt and saw. So often, when we meditate on the end, we think about it without God, allowing fear to creep in and steal our hope. But, no matter what happens, our promise is: *"Be strong and courageous. Do not be afraid or terrified because of them, for the LORD your God goes with you; he will never leave you nor forsake you"* (Deuteronomy 31:6).

# PART 2

## DISCOVERING A NEW MINDSET ABOUT GRIEF AND SUFFERING

# CHAPTER 7

## LOOKING AND SEEING THE BEAUTY FOR ASHES

> *"God answers Habakkuk by saying, "Look among the nations! See! Be astonished! Wonder! For I am doing something in your days—you would not believe it if you were told."*[29]

Several days after our house fire, I dug through the ashes of what used to be our home, looking for anything familiar. I'm searching for comfort in… well, anything. I feel like a girl looking at the sun but unable to feel its warmth.

The fire, of course, comes unexpectedly on a Thursday in the middle of the day. Still, grief has already been a familiar friend— familiar with the helplessness and the desperate need to find anything that would bring comfort and hope. In some strange way, digging through the remains of our home is my search for that comfort and hope today.

I feel waves of emotions as I sift through the ashes, hoping to discover a new dream to hold on to. But all I can see in front of me are unanswered prayers. I am heartbroken. Then, like a light in the darkness, I see a Christmas soap dispenser. It may be just a soap dispenser, but to

---

[29] Habakkuk 1:5, AMP

me, it's a tangible reminder of God's goodness and faithfulness that there can still be a spark of hope even in the ashes.

A reminder of the Presence of God.

It isn't material possessions I search for in these ashes, but hidden valuable treasures buried within the ruins. You don't think about how valuable things are until they're gone. It's easy to say you wouldn't be sad if you lost all your possessions as long as your loved ones were safe. After all, they're your most treasured possessions! That's true, but items become treasures over the years—nothing of real monetary value, but things that mean the world to you. I'm still incredibly grateful for the fireman who spent several hours pulling photos, my grandma's old journal, and even books he thought I might want out of the fire. Those things of no real "material" value bring comfort.

Here is some of what I lost in that fire:

All the journals I kept filled with thoughts and feelings over the years.

Handwritten letters between my husband and me.

All the books I collect and read to the children over the years.

A collection of Christmas ornaments, each with a story.

The assortment of drawings and homemade cards from the kids.

Every dance costume from my daughter's recitals.

My cozy sweater shirt I've had since college.

And don't get me started on all the old Bibles with notes and underlining throughout. While sorting through the debris, I feel the weight of loss and the ache of what once was.

Yet, in the desolation, I feel a flicker of hope.

An old figurine my grandmother gave me before she passed away emerges. Parts of it seem ruined from the flames. As I dust it off, admiring its beauty, I think about how God loves the not-so-perfect parts of us and how this figurine represents my broken parts, and God still thinks of how beautiful I am! He loves us despite our brokenness and sees our beauty, even when it is not so obvious.

As I pick up each imperfect, charred item, I see the remnants of what the fire destroyed and the redeeming future. There's beauty in the mess. As I ponder this thought, I wonder how God can take our broken pieces and create something even more beautiful than before.

I find myself in God's presence in the middle of the ashes of what once were my hopes and dreams–clinging to the debris. You see, He doesn't just remove all the debris and throw it into the garbage.

There's beauty hidden in the ashes.

Isaiah 61:3 says He promises us *"a crown of beauty instead of ashes."* I love what the Message version says, *"...give them bouquets of roses instead of ashes, messages of joy instead of a languid spirit. Rename them "Oaks of Righteousness" planted by God to display His glory."*

Transformation awaits us in the depths of our brokenness. Instead of being left with ashes, we'll receive bouquets of roses! Friend, God uses it all.

I know it's hard. Nothing about grief and trauma is easy. Our minds can't fathom how God will use the brokenness of our lives, but ashes placed in the hands of God are redeemed and remade.

When our souls are weary and our spirits weak in the darkest moments, God reaches out to us with tender love and compassion. He gathers the fragments of our shattered dreams and exchanges them for bouquets of roses, symbolizing beauty, love, and new beginnings. He infuses our mourning with joy, breathing life into our weary hearts.

Nothing disqualifies us from God's love. God can and will transform the broken and discarded parts of our lives and make them into something beautiful. God crowns us with beauty that reveals His glory and brings joy. This divine transformation is not limited to a mere superficial change but runs deep within the very core of our being.

God's love and grace have renamed us "Oaks of Righteousness," purposefully planted to bear witness to His glory and radiate His light in a world desperate for hope. It is not our past mistakes or the ashes of our brokenness that define us.

**85**

Beauty for ashes represents God's redemptive power (Isaiah 61:3). Many trials will come. Still, God makes it clear it will all return to dust (Ecclesiastes 3:20). Ashes are displayed on people's heads as a sign of grief (Joshua 7:6). Job repented in ashes (Job 42:6). Sodom and Gomorrah became nothing but ashes (2 Peter 2:6). Ashes throughout the Bible remind us that life's debris produces humility and brings about renewal.

God promises beauty for ashes… but the ashes are still part of our story. God doesn't act like they never existed.

In my desperation to not hurt, I realized I threw water on things that needed to burn. To see the beauty of ashes, I believed faith involved doing everything possible to extinguish the fire. In reality, faith is putting down the water pail and allowing things to burn that need to burn, believing God will bring beauty out of ashes even if the fire rages on for longer than we want it to.

Life's debris is scattered around me, and I'm trying to catch it all, hoping it will all come together again. Despite our grief and brokenness, ashes throughout the Bible remind us that our humility can bring about renewal, allowing us to come away from our trials with newfound strength and hope. Even though it's hard, He reforms us, making us into another version of ourselves through our brokenness.

There is a divine exchange where beauty emerges from the ruins of our lives.

Continuing my search through the ashes, I see the true treasure is not in the lost things but in God's redeeming plan. Amidst the ashes, I find the seeds of hope and renewal. Even in the darkest moments, a glimmer of light awaits a spark.

We tend to reject the very season in which God desires to unveil beauty because of the difficulties, unfilled longings, and obstacles in our path. We convince ourselves no beauty could possibly be within this mess. Slowly, I'm learning to see beauty in life's shattered and broken parts. God loves us so much that He would never leave it this way. Instead, He reforms us and our situations through the broken pieces.

Feeling discouraged among the ashes, I hear a voice whisper, "For I am doing something in your days—you would not believe it if you were told." I take this to mean that even though the ashes of my destroyed home surround me, something beautiful is still unfolding. I find strength in this promise of hope and begin to look around me for signs of life and beauty.

Habakkuk is an uncommon book of the Bible to study, but Habakkuk was a prophet asking similar questions to us. The prophets throughout the Bible spoke God's word to His people, making declarations of salvation and judgment, urging everyone to obey God's word. However, Habakkuk shares his concerns with God, giving voice to our struggles and wrestling. The things God allowed to happen didn't make sense to Habakkuk, and Habakkuk made it clear he was not happy.

Burdened by the world around him, Habakkuk wrote, *"God, how long do I have to cry out for help before you listen? How many times do I have to yell, "Help! Murder! Police!" before you come to the rescue? Why do you force me to look at evil, stare trouble in the face day after day?"*[30]

Habakkuk accused God of being silent, and God replied by warning Habakkuk that he was looking for answers in all the wrong places. *"Look at the nations, look—be utterly astounded! Something is going on in your day that you would not believe even if you were told."*

The Amplified Bible says, *"Look among the nations! and See! Be astonished! Wonder!"* (Habakkuk 1:5).

Look. See. Be astonished. Wonder. These four actions tell Habakkuk what to do.

I repeat these words as I sift through the ashes: *"Look. See. Be astonished. Wonder."*

God's invitation to look, see, be astonished, and wonder opens my spiritual senses to what He is doing among the ashes. God invites the prophet to see what He is doing in the chaos and confusion. He asks him to pay attention to the details and be amazed. God is always at work, even

---

[30] Habakkuk 1:1-3, MSG

amidst our darkest moments.

God is saying, "I hear you. You're focusing on your problems. However, I want you to see what I see."

God beckons us to keep our eyes on what He is doing rather than what we think He SHOULD be doing. God hears our prayers, understands our disappointment, and invites us into His perspective. Looking at broken promises is far easier than looking for the hidden beauty. God reminds us that He is actively working in our lives. Shifting focus on the beauty, rather than the broken promises we've experienced, allows us to see His presence. As we shift our focus, we can trust and rely upon Him to provide us hope and joy.

In our most profound anguish, it is easy to perceive pain as an overwhelming force ready to consume us. From our limited vantage point, it can feel like suffering has the power to tear us away from the very presence of God.

When we step back from the anguish of our situation, we gain a different perspective. We know from God's word that He grants Satan only a limited reach—a length of rope, if you will. It is enough rope to allow the enemy to weave his destructive schemes but *never* enough to sever our connection with God.

Even though the pain may assail us, it is essential to remember that God's presence remains steadfast. Today, He invites us to look, see, and be filled with astonishment and wonder!

Today, I received a surprise message of encouragement from a friend at the perfect moment. These small gestures of kindness often bring me joy and serve as reminders that God is active in our lives. My friend refers to them as "God winks," suggesting they're subtle signs of God's presence and love, particularly during difficult times. It's a comforting notion that even in times of suffering, God's hand is at work in mysterious ways.

I may not understand why I'm going through these trials, but God is with me and working in ways I can't see. These "God winks" are little reminders of His presence and love in difficulty.

God is greater than our suffering and always provides comfort and hope. We see this through the little things He does, like those "God winks." Moments of joy and peace may seem small, but they're powerful reminders of God's love and that He is with us even in the darkest times. They serve as a backdrop against which the grace and strength of God shine even brighter.

Even though, right now, we can't imagine a life without grief and suffering, God continues to weave a masterful symphony in the intricate dance between darkness and light. God's purposes always prevail. Suffering is a testament to our human spirit's resilience and the persistent presence of God's love. Though the pain may strive to tear us apart from God, it cannot sever the eternal bond we share with Him!

We stand on hope with unwavering faith until we see another side of grief, embracing the vulnerability that comes with acknowledging the harsh realities of life while staying rooted in the knowledge that God's power surpasses all trials. As we navigate the depths of our pain, let's trust that God's infinite wisdom guides every step of our journey, leading us toward a future where we've created a new normal within the suffering.

I know you may feel stuck, but ultimately, the rope given to the enemy becomes his undoing, and you *will* feel relief someday. God's eternal plan always prevails! We emerge from despair stronger, more resilient, and more intimately connected to the God of all hope and healing. And all the pain, suffering, anger, numbness, and confusion will not be your constant companion.

Growth and learning exist in childhood innocence, where wonder and curiosity intertwine. It is a realm where little hands reach out, eager to explore the world around them, and mistakes and mishaps become valuable teachers on life's journey. The same compassion and understanding we offer a child, we can provide to ourselves now. Acknowledge and celebrate the progress you make, no matter how small. Recognize the steps you take towards healing as you embrace your journey. Just as we celebrate a child's courage to try something new, to stumble, and then rise again, we can celebrate our bravery in embracing challenges and stepping into the unknown. We can recognize growth as a path filled with twists and turns. Mistakes are not signs of weakness but stepping stones to better knowing God.

Celebrating the wins helps us see the beauty among the ashes. For example, I started expressing gratitude for small steps forward, such as getting out of bed when feeling down. A journal now sits on my night stand to jot down "God winks." Each time I write one down, I know He's still working. We open ourselves to profound growth and self-compassion by embracing our imperfections in this time of grief and seeing the beauty in the broken.

A little over forty-five minutes after leaving Cabo San Lucas, our guide pulls over onto the roadside in the middle of the desert to an oasis. In the vast expanse of the desert, where the scorching sun beats down relentlessly and the winds whip up sand, a hidden, unexpected place of renewed hope exists in the most unlikely of spaces. My forty-year-old self stands looking down at this natural phenomenon with so many thoughts running through my mind. I don't want to move. My soul soaks up every moment.

Do the other tourists feel it, too? Overcome? Awestruck and captivated by His glory?

Picture it: a scene where the dry land and cactus stretch endlessly, their ridges and curves etched by the wind. With its unforgiving terrain, this land, the desert, tests the limits of endurance with its vast emptiness.

Suddenly, a glimmer catches my eye—a mirage of greenery and life that seems almost surreal. With each step closer, the air becomes more relaxed, and the scent of damp earth dances upon the wind! And there, like a secret whisper among the dunes, emerges an oasis that nourishes the body and soul.

Within the oasis, a profound stillness reigns. The rustling of leaves, the gentle babble of a small crystal-clear stream, and the chorus of birdsongs create a symphony of serenity. Lush foliage and vibrant blooms paint the landscape, contrasting the desolation beyond its borders. Time seems to pause, allowing weary souls to find refuge and restoration.

As I stand taking it all in, I remember my life's journey—this place is further proof that even in the most barren moments, there is the possibility of encountering unexpected beauty and peace. This real-life oasis proves the power of looking beyond the deserts of life to seek out the hidden places that can rejuvenate and inspire.

In the oasis, the world's weight lifts, and the layers of weariness disappear. I remember that a sovereign and creative God still holds our hardships. We can let go of the masks and the burdens we carry and immerse ourselves in the healing embrace of God's glory.

The oasis's resilience proves how life can thrive even in the most challenging conditions. Just as the oasis sustains life in the desert, we, too, can discover resilience within God's presence!

We can seek out our oases—those places, both external and internal, where we can replenish our spirits and find peace within life's challenges. In our desperate times, we can cultivate a mindset that embraces the oasis within, where vulnerability becomes a source of strength, and the barrenness of our trials transforms into fertile ground for growth.

Since we are image bearers of Christ, within each of us lies the potential to be an oasis—a sanctuary for ourselves and others. By nurturing our resilience, tending to our emotional and spiritual well-being, and extending compassion to those we encounter on our journey, we create ripples of hope that can transform deserts into fertile land.

Life throws sorrow and heartache at us, but if we can find beauty, we can live through it. Each moment and each experience has shaped me into who I am today. I stand here, in this vulnerable space, reflecting on the journey that has brought me to this moment.

Some chapters in my life have left indelible marks on my soul. Losing my father, enduring the devastation of the fire, navigating relationships, and witnessing my son battle addiction are some of my life's heartbreaking moments. But I've begun to train my eyes to see God's handy work within these moments, which carved a resilient pathway, strengthening my spirit and expanding my capacity for empathy and understanding.

I am not the same person I was when those significant events unfolded. I've shed layers of old beliefs. I've cleansed my spirit and let go of the weight of what no longer serves me. The person I am today is a tapestry of scars and stories, each etched upon my being, shaping my perspective, deepening my compassion, and awakening my inner strength.

In the face of adversity, I have discovered reservoirs of resilience I never knew existed.

Life is a masterpiece in progress. I witness my transformation, the peeling back of layers of my being, and embracing the ever-unfolding chapters of my story. I am now open to the lessons life offers and the wisdom hidden within the twists and turns of the journey.

With vulnerability as our guide and hope as our compass, we can enter the unknown, knowing we won't emerge as the same person. Each moment is a stepping stone toward the person we ultimately will become.

I've changed. Life has changed, and I can now celebrate the profound beauty that lies within this constant evolution. Each experience has gifted me with newfound strength, courage, and wisdom, no matter how difficult. As I continue to write my story, I honor the person I once was, the person I am now, and the person I am becoming.

Suffering casts its shadow but cannot extinguish the light that shines through the cracks of our brokenness. In these very moments, when we find ourselves in the depths of pain, we have been given the opportunity to witness the miraculous handiwork of God. As a delicate flower blooms in the most unexpected places, so does God's beauty flourish in our struggles. A fragile blossom's resilience is a testament to our strength to endure and rise above the challenges.

When we open our hearts and train our eyes to see, we'll uncover God's beauty in the tender touch of a loved one, the comforting embrace of a friend, or the gentle whisper of nature's melodies. We'll witness His beauty in others, acts of kindness and compassion, and the unwavering hope in each other's souls, and we'll be able to capture these God winks daily.

In times of suffering, stay connected to God by cultivating a deep and intimate relationship through prayer, meditation, and studying His Word. Seek His guidance, strength, and comfort as you navigate the transformation journey discussed in the upcoming chapters of this book, where we delve into discovering a new mindset about grief and suffering.

As we do, we'll discover God's peace, lean on His strength, and trust His unwavering love. We'll witness His beauty unfold like a breathtaking masterpiece, revealing the intricate brushstrokes of grace and the hues of redemption that flow through every aspect of our lives.

As you open your eyes and hearts to the beauty in our suffering, you'll learn to find gratitude for the gifts of grace in your life. You can slowly become a beacon of light, embracing the problematic process because one day, you will illuminate the path for others to discover the beauty ahead.

Remember, the journey from brokenness to beauty is unique for each individual. Be patient and kind to yourself along the way. Trust that God works in and through your life, bringing beauty and hope.

As I continue to walk and pray, I remember suffering is an invitation to experience more of God. If life went as planned, I wouldn't have the spiritual eyes to Him in new ways.

He's there in the middle of the ashes of life. He's there even when you're doing it all wrong. Trust that He will make all things new.

## DIGGING DEEPER:

1. Think of a time when you felt broken or experienced deep despair. How did you cope with that situation, and did you eventually find beauty emerging from the ashes?

2. This chapter discusses God's redemptive power, turning our brokenness into something beautiful. Reflect on a situation where you struggled to see any positive outcome. How does divine redemption challenge your perspective on suffering and adversity? In what ways can you shift your mindset toward God's redemption?

3. Trusting God during immense pain and uncertainty can be incredibly challenging. Are there specific practices, scriptures, or experiences that help you trust in God's promise to replace ashes with beauty?

# CHAPTER 8

## IT'S OKAY TO WRESTLE

> *"If God does what you think he should do, trust him. If God doesn't do what you think he should do, trust him. If you pray and believe God for a miracle and he does it, trust him. If your worst nightmare comes true, believe he is sovereign. Believe he is good."* [31]

I turn off the main road onto the windy back road toward the property of our new house. It has been a year since the fire, and I check the progress of the new build daily. Progress is slow. Everything has been taking longer since COVID. It's a struggle to get supplies, and workers are nowhere to be found. Our family is weary of living in the in-between. We are thankful that just days after the fire, our small community generously supplied nearly everything necessary to make our new rental feel like home. But now, we find ourselves in our second rental because the first one unexpectedly sold, and this new place doesn't feel like home.

Waves of mourning come at unexpected times, often catching me off guard. On this particular day, the grief of life feels extra heavy and lonely. My mom's cancer has reappeared in her hip bone, and to say I am mad at God is an understatement. We aren't on speaking terms at the moment. Still, a small voice inside me says, don't worry; God can handle it. *Why*

---

[31] Craig Groeschel, *The Christian Atheist: Believing in God But Living as If He Doesn't Exist* (Grand Rapids: Zondervan, 2010).

*does that feel so cliche right now?*

Douglas is wrapping up his ninety days at the second rehab, and we have yet to tell more than a few people about his struggle with addiction. Shame holds me captive, and I'm not ready to unravel the shame. There are places we must walk alone, right? Even in the struggles, our family's world keeps spinning—school, homework, football, basketball, dance, cheer, bedtime, discipline, and carpools anywhere and everywhere. When your world falls apart, and everything and everyone carries on with life as if nothing happened, it can take some adjusting. It is like watching life happen on a TV screen.

And several times a day, a question rattles around... *Why me?*

The Bible is clear that storms will come. As Jesus nears His time to be betrayed, arrested, and crucified, He addresses His disciples, saying, "*In the world, you will have tribulation. But take heart; I have overcome the world*" (John 16:33). His words are not tentative, using "might" or "if."

The conjunction "*but take heart*" strongly strings together His spoken words. My heart is still snagged and bruised despite His assurance that He has overcome the world. Overcoming the world seems lofty and far off. My mind comprehends, but my heart questions.

Where's the continuous, daily, tangible proof that He'll never stop showing up?

God commands the storms to be still, and quiet waters are a welcome relief after going through hell. Yet calm isn't sufficient; I yearn for stability, a place to confidently put my trust. These thoughts occupy my mind as I drive and sing along to worship music. A specific line from the song captures my attention: "Your goodness is running after me."

As the line repeats, I yell at God with tears running down my face, "Your goodness is not running after me! Your goodness has not been good to my family. You have not been good to Douglas. Everyone seems to have prayers answered but us.! My prayers are just hitting a brick wall!"

Shocked and simultaneously relieved, my ugly is now exposed. By embracing this transparency, I can rebuild my relationship with God on a foundation of honesty and sincerity.

Frederick Buechner once said, "If you don't have doubts, you're either kidding yourself or asleep. Doubts are the ants in the pants of faith. They keep it alive and moving."[32]

I can't explain it.

A complete peace sweeps over me. It's as if God was waiting for me to voice my frustration. I melt into a puddle of tears when I arrive at the house. Nothing magical happens on the outside. God didn't perform a miracle, and my struggles didn't magically disappear, but God provided a peace that surpasses all understanding. (Philippians 4:6).

Letting go of the shame and guilt of wrestling with God is difficult. You may be questioning God's goodness or asking "why."

Is questioning God even allowed?

Job asked the question "why" sixteen times. Questions and doubts brought to the feet of Jesus don't drive us away from God; they draw us closer to Him. Wrestling through the Scriptures and seeking the Truth draws our hearts closer to His.

The Bible contains story after story of people who wrestled with God through challenging circumstances. Take Elijah, the prophet.

In 1 Kings 19, we find Elijah frustrated with God—wrestling. After years of being utterly devoted to God, he ran out of fight. Obedient and determined to please God, Elijah repeatedly brought the Word of the Lord to the Israelites with seemingly no success. Elijah stood strong in the Lord countless times, never cowering to the people's opposition. Never taking no for an answer, he even condemned Israel's wicked King Ahab, Queen Jezebel, and their sons!

In 1 Kings 18:17, Elijah spoke boldly and confronted King Ahab with great courage and confidence in the Lord. He challenged Ahab and the false prophets to a duel between their god, Baal, and his God. On

---

[32] Frederick Buechner, *Wishful Thinking: A Theological ABC* (New York: Harper and Row, 1973).

that day, 450 Baal prophets stood against Elijah. Bold in his challenge, Elijah believed wholeheartedly in the power of his God. He knew that if he could prove the might of his God by making the Baal prophets look foolish, it would be a significant victory in the eyes of the people.

And Elijah did just that. Baal's 450 prophets were like a squad of champions... except the skies don't respond. Despite the prophets' fervent prayers and sacrifices, there was silence. But a consuming fire descended upon Elijah when he prayed, proving the power and might of his God!

Seems like a miracle to me. Elijah's prayers were answered with power, while Baal's 450 prophets went unanswered.

The next turn of events was different from what Elijah might have expected. Despite his pleas, the Israelites continued on their path of wickedness and idolatry.

Wait. What? Elijah obeyed the Lord, and the people continued in their wickedness.

Queen Jezebel sent a messenger to Elijah with the message, *"May the gods deal with me, be it ever so severely if by this time tomorrow, I do not make your life like that of one of them"* (1 Kings 19:2).

Elijah came to a broom tree, sat under it, and prayed that he might die.

In his next breath, he asked God to take away his life, saying, *"It is enough; now, O Lord, take away my life, for I am no better than my fathers"* (vs 4-5). He decided that he would rather die than face the wrath of Jezebel.

Elijah's broom tree isn't all that different from our unexpected places. Elijah was not only physically and emotionally exhausted, but he was also spiritually exhausted, begging God to take his life. If we're sincere, we've all felt pretty similar to Elijah.

All our praying and trying just leads us to more disappointment and heartache. We collapse into bed with nothing else to give. We feel frustrated and defeated by the unanswered prayers and disappointments, causing weariness and exhaustion to plague most of our days. Our heart's desire is for comfort.

In frustration, we want to scream, *"Enough, Lord,"* just like Elijah.

I admire Elijah's honesty with the Lord, and God met his honesty with comfort! Instead of a rebuke, God offered comfort. Elijah fell asleep only to awaken with food and water at his feet and an angel telling him to *"Arise and eat"* (vs. 5). He ate and drank and fell asleep again. *"And the angel of the Lord came again a second time, touched him, and said, "Arise and eat, for the journey is too great for you. And he arose and ate and drank"* (1 King 19:7-8).

God didn't meet Elijah's depression and desperation with a lecture. He didn't tell Elijah he needed to pray more or that he was wrong for feeling the way he did. Instead, God's angel offered Elijah the companionship and consolation he desperately needed. The angel's message was simple and comforting: his depression was not a punishment but a reminder of God's deep love and presence.

Like Elijah, we need rest and nourishment for our souls and bodies in the wrestling and questioning. We don't need to be afraid to come to God boldly. There will be no rebuke, guilt trip, or work-harder lecture. God touched Elijah, let him sleep, and fed him twice. His problems may not have ended, and his heart may have still been hurting, but he could continue forward. We need people, and we need to be people who hold each other when we are sad and feed us when we're too tired to do it ourselves.

In verse 10, Elijah told God, *"I have been very jealous for the Lord, the God of hosts."* He further states people are seeking to take his life. When the prophet witnessed horrible sins, he didn't blast social media or lobby the government. Instead, he yelled at God about it! And God did something remarkable. God revealed Himself in a whisper. We're looking for God to speak in neon lights and God's longing to meet us in the quiet. Showing up to God with questions and doubts allows Him to reveal Himself to us in a new way. One thing to remember in grief and trauma is that the enemy's voice is loud, and God's is a whisper.

Our questions cultivate a deeper trust in the One who's overcome the world; *"take heart."*

God didn't make Elijah's problems go away. He did quite the opposite: *"Go, return on your way to the wilderness of Damascus"* (1 King 19:15). God didn't alter Elijah's mission in life. Instead, He gifted him with his presence, the manna he needed to continue.

God doesn't always provide a clear path out of the valley, but He always gives us a way through.

The death of a loved one can shift the focus of our prayers. After my dad graduated from Earth to Heaven, my prayer life changed. His death broke something within me—that happens when you believe for a miracle, and it doesn't transpire this side of heaven.

Unknowingly, for most of my life, I approached God as a genie in a bottle. You know—rub the lamp, ask for a wish, and *voila!*—the wish is granted.

Up until my dad's death, this worked. No sudden losses or sickness. Love story marriage. My husband attended the medical school of his choice, graduating with honors. He stepped through a wide-open door to his chosen residency program, keeping us near family. He joined the military to pay for medical school and never deployed. Miraculously, my son's half a heart beats strong, avoiding the ongoing medical care most of these kids need—literal years of escaping tragedy and suffering—one open door after another. Opportunity continued knocking on our door, making me believe my prayers shook heaven.

I bought the lie that your actions are essential to answered prayers, and my relationship with God became transactional instead of intimate.

It is a slippery slope to believe that reading the Bible, chanting specific words, and following the law guarantees your prayers will be answered.

When you find yourself at a grave site, facing another cancer diagnosis or another unexpected situation, you begin questioning if you even *believe* in healing. Or prayer, for that matter.

I'm wrestling with God— like David—with all my emotions.

My distorted "genie-in-a-bottle" theology led me to believe that if I behaved well, He'd love me and respond to my prayers. This mindset held up until my father passed away. Eventually, you have to confront your beliefs when faced with suffering.

Do you remember the movie *Aladdin?*

If you recall, the Genie's only job was to advance the agenda of his master, Aladdin. Granting only his master's requests, never once did the Genie consider how these wishes could impact the purpose and plans of others.

The "genie-in-bottle" mindset is selfish. We've bought into a materialistic belief that *we* are the story's center, not God.

Except the last time I checked, God's greatest desire is to glorify His name.

Dabbling in the notion of God as a genie in a bottle carries a double-edged sword. When our hopeful prayers go unanswered, we're left shattered, questioning the strength of our faith.

I crawl into bed feeling like a failure on more nights than I can count. These feelings of loss hinge on the belief that if I did it all right, my genie in the sky would snap his fingers to grant all my requests.

How did I become so convinced that following Jesus would provide an escape from sorrow? And why do I keep pursuing the myth that everything will be okay if I follow some formula? This mindset is dangerous.

God is *not* a genie in a bottle. As C.S. Lewis wrote, *"God does not exist for the sake of man. Man does not exist for his own sake."*[33]

Experiencing the pain of prayers going unanswered can harden our hearts toward God. Before my dad's death, I took God's grace and blessings for granted, assuming He would fulfill my desires on my schedule. I unknowingly tied His goodness to His actions in my life – if He blessed me, He was good; if He held back, He seemed untrustworthy. My trust became conditional, and I overlooked His grace and goodness

---

[33] C.S. Lewis, *The Problem of Pain* (New York: HarperOne, 2015).

in every aspect of life, whether good, bad, or ugly.

For years, my faith fluctuated between outward surrender on Sundays and inner doubt throughout the week. I'd raise my hands in surrender during church on Sundays, but the rest of the week was characterized by self-reliance and forging my own path rather than trusting in the Spirit. Over time, my faith started to transform.

"Miracles don't always make faith. Tangible proofs don't guarantee trust. On the other hand, suffering, loss, difficulty, questions, wrestling, and the oceanic grace and unflinching presence do. And, perhaps, the fact that grace and nearness show up in these kinds of places is, despite us, the real miracle."[34]

Can I be honest? Hashing out my questions for the world to see makes me nervous. God is so vast that I can't pretend to understand Him completely. In Philippians, the Apostle Paul instructs us to *"Work out your salvation with fear and trembling"* (Philippians 2:12).

So here we are, wrestling with hard questions from a place of humility. I'm not attempting to force brilliant answers to complex questions. But maybe I'm on to something, or I'm entirely off the mark. I know one thing: I'm a fellow pioneer walking this faith journey alongside you. Perhaps my questioning will help your questioning. One thing is for sure: you need to keep wrestling after you put this book down, and so do I because "Hard questions are invitations to stand on the foundation of what you already know about God."[35] —in the confusion and suffering, we have the assurance that He won't abandon us.

The truth is that *Jesus* should set the priority and agenda for our prayers. This life we live is for His glory, not our own! Over the last few years, I desperately wanted to control God's glory, directing Him on how He could receive the most glory. He was good only if He saved me and my family from suffering and pain. I wanted a fairy-tale ending, kind of God.

---

[34] Michele Cushatt, *Relentless: The Unshakeable Presence of a God Who Never Leaves* (Grand Rapids: Zondervan, 2019), 34.
[35] Dannah Gresh, *Habakkuk: Remembering God's Faithfulness When He Seems Silent* (Chicago: Moody Publishers, 2020).

I prayed, *"God, heal my mom for your glory."*

When God miraculously heals, His glory shines brightly for all to see. But what about those times when His divine intervention doesn't come in the form of miraculous healing? Isn't His glory just as evident when He grants us the strength to navigate life's darkest valleys?

*"When he heard this, Jesus said, 'This sickness will not end in death. No, it is for God's glory so that God's son may be glorified through it'"* (John 11:4).

Was God's glory not seen in my dad's death? Is God's glory not seen in life's messy, not-so-perfect places? Is His glory only seen in the well-orchestrated-put-together parts of our life?

I dive into Scripture in the early mornings, trying to learn about God's glory.

> *"Holy, Holy, Holy is God of the Angel-Armies.*
> *His bright glory fills the whole earth."[36]*
> *To the one who comes near me,*
> *I will show myself holy;*
> *Before all the people, I will show my glory.[37]*

Lazarus's death and subsequent resurrection had an ultimate purpose: it was for the glory of God (John 11:4; cf. 14:13). Peter's death also shared this purpose (John 21:19). Paul points out that God chooses, adopts, redeems, and seals believers *"to the praise of the glory of his grace"* (Eph. 1:6, 12, 14).

Glory is God's character on display. No matter the outcome, His glory is on display through the power of the Holy Spirit moving through.

I remember a kind, loving lady from hospice walking into my parent's kitchen days before my dad's passing. Dad lies in the recently dropped-off hospital bed in the den as we discuss the end of his life. Tears well up in my eyes; knowing that the end is drawing near, I'm just not ready. I quickly called my sister since it would take her a whole day of travel to

---

[36] Isaiah 6:3 MSG
[37] Leviticus 10:3 MSG

get to us.

We do everything needed to make Dad comfortable. He didn't talk or eat that last day. He simply waits for my sister to arrive. The sound of the grandchildren running in and out fills the house throughout the day. Then, at 3 a.m., he experiences victory over his cancer in the arms of Jesus. His wish to die at home in Mississippi, surrounded by his three girls, is granted. My mom, sister, and I held hands, praying as he graduated into Heaven. A peace I'd never experienced (and still haven't again) filled the room that day. Without a doubt, God's glory is on display. For the first time in my dad's life, he is whole and healed.

My uncle sent me a photo of my dad and myself a few hours after my dad passed away. The picture was taken at the airport over a year ago when we were saying goodbye after a visit, embracing each other tightly. In that hug, I could feel his profound love for me. I imagined my dad entering the embrace of Jesus just like that, enveloped by God's love, and hearing God say to him, "Everything is alright now." My friend, this is God's glory on display!

If the glory of God is the manifested beauty of His holiness, then His glory is the going public of His holiness. It's His holiness on display, painting a canvas for all to see. In other words, the glory of God is the holiness of God made manifest.

The work of a good and kind Father is not dependent on earthly circumstances.

**Habits to Live by When Wrestling with God**

I am far from perfect and weak in the waves of life's storms. I envy others who have smoothly launched their teens into college and seemingly seem to navigate life without struggles. The talk of prayers being effortlessly answered only rubs salt in my wounds. Most days, reading becomes daunting, especially while wrestling with God and navigating the drowning weight of grief. It's crucial I find a way to feast on the Word. Whatever it takes, it's essential to open the Word and align with its truths rather than relying solely on podcasts, sermons, or others' words.

During sleepless nights, I turn to earbuds, listening to someone read

God's Word. In daylight, I write His Word on notecards and scatter them around the house. Praying out loud, I cling to verses written on cards.

As my brain turns to mush, it makes it challenging to remember even simple things. Scribbling a few words in my journal is an accomplishment on a good day, and remembering to feed myself feels like a victory. Beyond exhaustion, sleep eludes me, and comprehending the Bible seems impossible. The realization of how desperate I am for Living Water only dawns on me when my spirit feels completely dry. We aren't truly living if we deprive ourselves of the very thing that brings us life.

*"Are you tired? Worn out? Burned out on religion? Come to me. Get away with me, and you'll recover your life. I'll show you how to take a real rest. Walk with me and work with me—watch how I do it. Learn the unforced rhythms of grace. I won't lay anything heavy or ill-fitting on you. Keep company with me, and you'll learn to live freely and lightly."*[38]

Jesus acknowledges our weariness. He doesn't shame us, label it, or accuse us of not being faithful Christians. Instead, He invites us to rest. But it takes acknowledging our weariness. Jesus draws us to His heart. He isn't telling us to come when we have it all together or when our emotions are stable. He will carry us. God is in the losses and the questioning. The weariness is never an indication to try harder. The weariness is an invitation to experience more of Him. In the weariness, He meets us with the promise of hope and peace.

Close your eyes, take a deep breath, and on the exhale, say, "God is with me."

Being aware of God's presence keeps Satan from distracting us in the questioning. If we're not careful, inquisitiveness can lead us down a slippery slope if we don't saturate ourselves in the unchanging Word of God.

As I sit in the driveway of our rebuild, God pulls me in and surrounds me with His Presence. I turn toward Hope. I can live through the breaking. *Deep Breathe.* As I wrestle and ask questions, he serves as my safety net. Having immersed myself in Scripture over the years helps

---

[38] Matthew 11:28-30, MSG

me remember that even when things spin out of control, God doesn't. His love and faithfulness remain, no matter what the circumstance.

The journey of faith is not without its challenges and questions. Embrace the process of wrestling and seeking, knowing that God's love and faithfulness are constant, providing comfort and guidance along the way.

---

## DIGGING DEEPER:

1.  Acknowledge your weariness: Take a moment to recognize and validate it. Allow yourself to rest and find peace in Jesus, who understands and invites you to find rest in Him.

2.  Embrace the hard questions: Instead of avoiding or suppressing your questions, see them as invitations to deepen your understanding of God. Stand on the foundation of what you already know about Him and seek His guidance and wisdom in your confusion and suffering.

# CHAPTER 9

## UNMASKING SHAME

*"At the core of recovery is self-awareness. The most important phrases in trauma therapy are "Notice that" and "What happens next? Traumatized people live with seemingly unbearable sensations... Yet avoiding feeling these sensations in our bodies increases our vulnerability to being overwhelmed by them"*[39]

A week after dropping Douglas off at his second rehab, I lie in bed with excruciating pain in my abdomen. Mike drops me off at home thirty minutes after being diagnosed with bladder spasms in the doctor's office. Bladder spasms? Never in my life have I experienced something like this.

There are many layers of emotions, and the pain can be physical *and* emotional. Grief and trauma wreak havoc on the body and mind. Honestly, there were times I didn't know how I'd make it through the day other than through the grace of God. I endured physical, emotional, and spiritual symptoms, but no one warned me of the physical symptoms that came. Nobody talks about chronic insomnia, random bladder infections, stomach knots, headaches, sweating, or racing heartbeats (just to name a few out of a whole slew of physical symptoms that can occur from trauma).

---

[39] Bessel Van Der Kolk, MD, *The Body Keeps the Score* (New York: Penguin Books, 2014), 210.

Trauma in our brain can majorly impact our psychological health. Our brains control and regulate our thoughts, behavior, and emotions. Trauma damage to the brain can affect cognitive processes, such as memory and problem-solving, and emotional processes, such as mood and motivation.[40]

Most of the time, suffering is that friend, forcing you to travel in directions you wouldn't otherwise explore. The reality is that my emotional pain is causing my body physical pain.

Every breath hurts.

Every part of my body aches.

Life has to keep moving forward. I don't have time to be sick. I don't want to be still because if I slow down, my mind begins to race with anxious thoughts.

And somehow, you keep going because the world won't stop just for you.

And people don't offer support like they would if your mental pain were a physical illness or death. I felt isolated by all the various forms of my suffering.

Can I accept that maybe God was using my bladder spasms as part of my journey to slow me down to look inward and learn from the pain rather than merely trying to escape it?

As I lie there observing the stillness and heaviness in the house, I can finally admit that my son has a problem with addiction, except shame quickly follows.

Shame for not noticing the symptoms earlier.

Shame at having failed to prevent Douglas's descent into addiction.

Shame for my love not being enough to save him.

Shame for having a child who has an addiction problem.

Shame for not praying hard enough to create the miracle I desperately

---

[40] van der Kolk, *The Body Keeps the Score*, 97.

longed for.

Shame snuffs out our identity in Christ and bullies us into believing we're unworthy of healing. If we are not careful, it will back us into a corner, convincing us to quit on God. Shame has the power to change the trajectory of our lives. It causes us to shrink from relationships, community, and even vulnerability, bullying us into believing feelings are wrong, which opens doors to anger, bitterness, and depression.

Shame keeps us stuck.

The waves of shame have diminished the joy of life. The "Jesus is enough for everything" mantra isn't cutting it. In the layers of shame, this question, "Did I not trust God enough?" arises.

Without knowing how the brain scientifically works, well-meaning Christian leaders counsel to stop taking medication and trust God, as if somehow taking medication prevents one from trusting God. It's all overwhelming.

"Lea, it's time to go back to counseling," a loving friend suggests.

About six months after the fire and at the peak of Douglas's addiction, I enter the counselor's office midmorning on a weekday. I arrive a few minutes before my appointment and sit in the waiting room, reflecting on how my counselor and I have covered a lot of ground over the last few years. I can't remember how I stumbled upon her practice. All I know is that her counseling skills helped me find the courage after my dad's death to speak Truth over the critical voice in my head. She's the encouragement I needed to try an antidepressant medication, which opened the door to gaining a better understanding of my mental health and finding ways to manage it.

Surprisingly, this little white pill has been critical to my healing. Unfortunately, there's so much shame wrapped around taking medication to ease the ongoing war within the mind. Since Christians often promise "Three Steps to ____" or "Have a New Kid by Friday!" Often taking medication implies a lack of faith.

Life, unfortunately, doesn't follow such simplistic rules.

Offering these assurances alienates those who attempt to meet all the standards but fall short, which in turn causes immense shame.

There's a stigma within the church community when it comes to counseling. But I'm here to tell you—counseling has been my healing grace in this healing journey.

Fast forward six months into Douglas's battle with addiction, and here I am, slowly untangling the knots inside me. It's a story of processing and healing. I'm still a work in progress. They're right when they say, "A wise therapist and a cup of joe can tackle pretty much anything life throws at you!"

Antidepressants (or any other kind of medications for mental health) are support tools, not quick-fix solutions. Just like doctors suggest a lifestyle change when prescribing cholesterol or diabetes medication, mental health medications are no different. They assist in the healing process. In my case, they helped clear my mind and change my internal dialogue from negative to positive.

Linda, my counselor, sees the burden weighing on my shoulders. I sink into the couch, wearing my emotions like a banner of sadness. Without delay, Linda asks me the loaded question, "How are you?"

I draw a deep breath and respond, "Not great, but I'm trying to make it through the day without crying in public - so that's something, right?"

I lean in, seeking guidance, "How do I navigate caring for myself, life, and my children?"

The day of the house fire marked a new era in my mothering journey. The seven of us dove headfirst into a sea of challenges, and I felt like a lifeguard desperately trying to rescue them while relentless waves pulled me farther from the safety of the shore.

Two years have passed in a whirlwind of losing and rediscovering each other. I've spent this time reminding myself to breathe, fearing that everything could crumble at any moment, while attempting to keep all the plates spinning—two years of busyness, trying to outrun the tidal wave of emotions.

Yet, during trauma, I'm learning how to be a mother in this season— because with trauma comes shame—it's an inevitable companion.

With grace, my therapist unfolds the connection between trauma and intense emotions like shame, guilt, and anger. These feelings cling stubbornly, stirring further distress and emotional turmoil. However, it's crucial to acknowledge them as a normal part of the healing process. Navigating these emotions is challenging yet essential. Patience and compassion pave the way to move through traumatic experiences with increased ease and resilience.

As a mom post-trauma, my prayers are a constant plea for my children to conquer their demons. Staying hopeful, even when faced with adversity, gives me the strength to prioritize love instead of withdrawing into apathy and hopelessness. I walk beside my children in their pain, allowing the trauma to carve their character. I support them in expressing their emotions in a healthy way by encouraging self-care activities such as journaling, listening to music, or taking a long walk to give them the breathing room they need.

Seated there, baring my emotions to my counselor, I sense a reluctance to share more, holding back questions, doubts, and untold stories. The burden of upholding a facade of normalcy weighs heavily, leaving me drained. Months of shuttling back and forth to visit Douglas at rehab, concealing our true destination from most friends by feeding them fabricated stories about his well-being. The shame of having a son grappling with addiction pushes me to wear the "I'm fine" mask. Unfortunately, the mask feels safer than shedding the shame and standing exposed. It serves as a refuge from the uncomfortable silence and the burden of being a parent with a struggling child.

As I face my counselor, I lay bare my struggles, realizing the isolation that has taken hold. Attempts to communicate with friends and family have fallen short, as they seem to stand on the other side of a glass wall, peering in, unable to comprehend my experience. Opening up to Linda, my voice quivers, and tears well up. I disclose the challenges I've faced in the past few months, including my reluctance to discuss Douglas's addiction with close friends and the overwhelming feeling of not deserving God's goodness and grace." Reflecting on the seventeen years of Douglas's life, I question if I could have been a better mother. It dawns on me that I feel unqualified to be a parent.

"Oh, Lea, you're wrapped in shame. That's not from God," she says.

There are many "what-ifs" with loss. It is easy to beat ourselves up wondering if we had done or not done this or that; maybe our story would have turned out differently. Our "what-ifs" can cause us to hit a brick wall, keeping us paralyzed and unable to move forward. Our unchecked *what-ifs* leave us exposed to shame and bitterness.

We can't allow our "what-ifs" to boss us around. Most of the time, we can't help the brokenness, and you certainly can't help how the story turns out. We wish we weren't bruised and broken this way, but the shame won't support healing. The shame and guilt only slam and smash against our knowledge of who God is.

Our world doesn't celebrate brokenness. Even a broken toy a child loves goes into the garbage. We often view our broken selves as broken toys—unusable and quickly replaceable. We feel the need to blend into the background and shrink from our gifts because nothing in our lives seems to be bearing fruit. Shame digs its claws into us, keeping us from our God-given identity.

I wonder if instead of asking ourselves, "What if I had done something differently?" we can reframe the question to "What can I do differently *now*?"

Walking out the doors of my counselor's office, I realize that just like there's no shame in letting tears come, there's no shame in processing the hurt or getting angry at your situation. Emotions are a gift and a reflection of the heart of God. After you release them, you can experience healing and wholeness. It's like taking the lid off a boiling pot—the steam escapes, releasing pressure and allowing what's inside to cool down.

In the same way, releasing emotions can help us find balance and peace.

Feeling emotions allows grace to pour inside of our souls. Without emotions, we become numb, and numbness cultivates bitterness, resulting in unplowable ground. It's okay some days to be unproductive, emotionally unavailable, and exhausted. It's okay to force a smile and then cry alone in your car. It's *all* okay because it's *all* part of the healing process. So, even in a dark place, it's important to remember that our emotions are necessary for recovery and shouldn't be dismissed.

What if we can extend grace instead of shame to ourselves for not pushing harder toward healing?

Jesus is our perfect example of validating emotions in suffering. In John 21, the disciples did the most logical thing after Christ's death:

Fish.

Simon Peter was the first to say, *"I'm going fishing." And the rest of the disciples followed, replying, "We're coming with you."*(vs 3).

After accompanying Jesus to His death and burial, the confused and worn-out disciples returned to their prior lives. Like many of us who feel lost and disoriented because life didn't go as planned, these men returned to the comfort of normal life to numb the pain, giving themselves some sense of normalcy. I can only imagine the *"what-ifs"* going through Peter's mind: "If only I hadn't denied Jesus. If only I had admitted to being His follower." Peter must have longed for a way to make up for his mistake.

A long night of fishing and not catching anything brought Peter face-to-face with Jesus, and he struggled to believe that Jesus was here in the flesh. Christ called from the shoreline, *"Cast the net on the right side of the boat, and you will find some"* (John 21:6). Jesus reminded Peter that, once again, he cannot find his way out of the darkness without Him.

In Peter's suffering came shame. Jesus invited him to experience abundant life despite the loss and the setback of denying Him. Jesus extended grace to Peter, showing us that although we may be in darkness, His love brings light and hope for a new beginning.

Jesus could have rebuked Peter, telling him he had no faith, or said, "How can you go back to fishing after all I've taught you? Don't you have any faith?" Instead, *"Jesus said to them, "Come and have breakfast."*(vs 12)

Jesus doesn't merely serve a meal. He invests the time to lovingly prepare it, locking eyes with His disciples to empathize deeply with their pain and disappointment. He goes the extra mile, kindling a fire to cook the fish and offering bread, fully aware that the Bread of Life is precisely what they need. His actions are an intimate understanding of their desperate yearning for peace and reassurance. *"When they got out on land, they saw a charcoal fire there, with fish laid out on it, and bread"* (John 21:9).

Through the simple act of preparing breakfast on the beach, Jesus reveals His compassionate nature and willingness to meet His disciples during their struggles. Rather than expecting them to overcome their discouragement and doubts immediately, He extends a gesture of understanding, allowing them to make a fresh start, renewed and encouraged by His grace and love.

In contrast to presenting a list of strict do's and don'ts or chastising them for their lapses in faith and return to old habits, Jesus chooses a path of comfort, grace, and shared presence. He goes so far as to invite Peter to contribute the fish he caught for the meal, emphasizing our collective role in the ongoing healing process.

It's over breakfast that Jesus addresses Peter's shame. Three times, Jesus asks him, *"Do you love me?"* He pokes at the wound to expose the shame Peter was internalizing. Jesus poked until Peter became irritated: *"You know that I love you"* (John 21:17). There it was… Peter's shame is exposed. Jesus brings to light what Peter tried to keep in the dark. *"Feed my sheep,"* Jesus said, extending grace to the shame and offering a new identity to preach the gospel. (vs 17)

Jesus replaced Peter's shame with hope, a powerful reminder that our past doesn't have to determine our future. Aren't you glad our past doesn't dictate our future?

With just a snap of a finger, miraculously, the fish could have been cooked and ready to go. Fast and Easy, prepared and ready to eat without the fire, just like when Christ fed the five thousand. Jesus knew they needed more than food. They needed His presence. They longed for Him to look them in the eye and speak Life. When Jesus fed the five thousand, He showed that He provided physical sustenance; with the disciples, Jesus offered comfort and assurance—something no one else could do. He listened, understood their hurts, and brought real love and hope into their lives.

Jesus doesn't always perform miracles, but He *always meets* us right where we are by entering our brokenness and sorrow with His comforting presence. He speaks peace and hope into our lives, reminding us that He is always with us and will never leave us.

"Real love takes vulnerability. Because 'vulnerability is the only bridge to build connection."[41] Vulnerability requires a willingness to be open and honest with God and one another without hiding behind masks. It takes sitting in uncertainty and silence without throwing around Christian clichés and quick-fix answers.

Real lovers know that scars are beauty marks reflecting God's goodness and that when we simply sit close and listen, we cultivate deep friendships. Shame poisons the hope that things can improve; identifying the shame allows us to move toward healing.

After that counseling appointment, attempting to move toward healing and crawl out from underneath the shame, I text a friend to say, "We may need more than an hour for lunch tomorrow. I have a lot to tell you."

We meet for lunch almost every Wednesday for months now, but I avoid discussing the struggle with Douglas's addiction. I know the time has come to share my part of the story (the other parts belong to my son since it's ultimately his story). As parents, we tread a fine line between what's ours to share and theirs to share. I need to be mindful of how much I share with my friend to ensure I respect his privacy.

The next day, we sit at a picnic table on the patio of a local restaurant, sipping cocktails. A slight breeze blows through my hair as I tuck my hands under my legs. I take a deep breath, and my heart feels like it will pound right out of my chest. I start to talk about Douglas, stuttering and stumbling over my words but continuing to speak with conviction. "Why is this so hard for me?" I think to myself. "Why am I afraid to disclose the truth?"

You don't have to wait to trust someone else to bear the suffering

---

[41] Brené Brown, *Braving the Wilderness: The Quest for True Belonging and the Courage to Stand Alone* (New York: Random House Publishing Group, 2017).

alongside you. Moving forward requires trusting a few friends with the darkest parts of your story. We can push on as hard as possible, but we'll lose hope without a few friends sharing the burden.

I begin with, "I've been lying to you about something." And for what feels like forever, I tell her as much as possible. I share how I feel inadequate and turn to addictive behaviors to cope with my difficult emotions.

I don't remember all I shared, but she listens willingly, not pointing fingers or offering answers. Instead, she helps carry my burden through prayer and the gift of her presence. Vulnerability sparks healing and forgiveness within me. This friend affirms my worth and mirrors the Father's heart of unconditional love.

I take off my mask.

When I finish sharing as much as possible:

Silence.

I sit there, stunned.

"Okay, so that's it?" she finally says. "Listen. Nothing you can say changes how I feel about Douglas, you, or Mike. I've been praying about this conversation and anticipating whatever you had to say."

Her words pierce me.

"Shame dies when stories are told in safe places."[42] We must name what we're carrying before we can experience freedom.

I didn't expect the conversation to release something inside me. But it did. I experienced a grace that penetrates my soul, allowing hope and forgiveness to unleash my chains of shame. It's like a ray of sunlight breaking through the storm clouds, illuminating the way forward. My friend reaches deep inside herself to understand me and holds the needed space. She graciously reminds me that our kids are not the products of our parenting.

---

[42] Ann Voskamp, *The Broken Way: A Daring Path Into the Abundant Life* (Grand Rapids: Zondervan, 2016).

Even though it may seem painful to open up, disclosing your truth to a few trusted friends can act as an anchor of strength and hope. Once I start trusting a few people with my story, I feel immense relief, knowing I don't have to face it alone.

Later that evening, Mike and I sat telling another couple about the hellish journey we'd been on. Our friends look us right in the eyes and say, "We still look up to you as parents." Their words are both a reminder and affirmation that I haven't done a terrible job as a parent despite all our troubles.

As we travel through life, we each carry our own story with unique twists and turns, joys and sorrows, triumphs and struggles. It can be easy to feel isolated as if no one understands our path. But the truth is, we're not meant to walk this journey alone. Instead, we were designed to support and uplift one another, to offer a listening ear, a gentle touch, a word of affirmation. We can make each other's journey slightly brighter through the gift of presence. And in turn, we receive the same gift from those who walk alongside us. We each have an individual journey, but together, we can find strength, comfort, and hope as we face life's ups and downs.

"Think of feeling safe enough with another person that without weighing words of measuring thoughts, you can pour yourself out, trusting that the other person will keep what is worth keeping and, with a breath of kindness, blow the rest away."[43]

Brenner calls this "soul friendship" a place where anything can be said or felt without criticism or fear of rejection. There's no shaming. There's no need to show up like anyone else but yourself. Instead, you're accepted for who you are and how you feel in this season of life. Soul friendships give you a sense of safety. It's a gift of love. It's creating space for others.

Not many people can listen and create space for the hard in life. Think how often you've been with someone who appears to be listening, but they check their phone once or twice. They're not listening; they're

---

[43] David G. Benner, *Sacred Companions* (Downers Grove, IL: InterVarsity Press, 2002), 48.

just trying to figure out what to say next. You can fake presence, but there is no faking empathy.

We can only be fully present to ourselves and others if we are fully present with God.

Sometimes, you need someone to sit in the darkness with you, with no promises of how this shall pass. No reminders of brighter days ahead. Just someone to share the dark space without condemnation. Just someone to make you feel loved and seen.

According to John 8:1-11, one day in the temple, the religious leaders dragged a woman caught in adultery before Jesus. She most likely stood half-clothed, with her head hanging low, as they quoted the law, *"Now in the law, Moses commanded us to stone such women. (vs 5)"*

I imagine shame and condemnation covered her like a dense haze on a warm summer night, unable to look anyone in the eye. I know this feeling all too well. God's conditional love, wrapped in shame and disappointment, deemed me unworthy for many years.

Jesus said, *"Let him who is without sin among you be the first to throw a stone at her (vs 7).* Aka, those who have it all together. He challenged the small-mindedness of the self-righteous religious leaders by saying, *"Go ahead, throw the first stone."*

So often, unknowingly, we're like those self-righteous religious leaders ready to throw stones with our "Christian advice." It is like trying to shoot an arrow in the dark—you may feel like you are doing something productive, but you are probably doing more harm than good without knowing the situation and not entering it with compassion.

Jesus did the unthinkable. He stooped down and wrote something in the dirt. What He wrote is a mystery, though many theologians have their ideas. Some say Jesus wrote the accusers' names, and others say He may have written the accusers' sins. But, I heard a pastor once preach that Jesus stooped down to look into the woman's eyes with love to say, "It's okay, my daughter. I love you."

Whatever He wrote doesn't matter because the beauty of the story remains the same. He never condemned her with shame. He didn't tell her to work harder or to pull herself together. He met her with Love.

With her sin exposed, this woman most likely experienced love and acceptance for the first time, and it gave her the courage to leave her mask of shame and guilt behind as Jesus spoke. *"Neither do I condemn you. Go from now on, do not sin anymore"* (John 8:11).

*"But now he has reconciled you by Christ's physical body through death to present you holy in his sight, without blemish and free from accusation"*— Jesus sees us through the eyes of love. Colossians 1:22

God's love is transformational. When we live in this love, fully accepted, we can remove the masks we've been wearing and be our true God-given selves. Brennan Manning writes, "While we love someone for what we find in him or her...Jesus loves men and women not for what he finds in them, but for what he finds in himself."[44]

For too long, I have been caught in the trap of restlessness, pretending to be someone I'm not. It's not about what we do or don't do; it's about how we love. I used to think I had to earn love and acceptance, but the truth is, it's already freely given to us. So, even amid grief and shame, God promises to complete the good work He began.

Our concept of a life lived for God can—in the end—be oh so different than what He intended for us. We act as if certain sins or struggles make us ineligible for grace, like depression, addiction, divorce, and all the other things that mark us as broken or weak. Often, we describe God's grace as an ocean, an endless expanse of love and mercy that washes over us regardless of how deep our failures or doubts might be. I wonder what would happen if we lived like we believed this.

There was a time when my deepest failures felt like they created a wall between me and God's love. No matter how hard I tried to swim, I could never reach the shore. But I'm learning that God's grace isn't a limited resource that only applies to certain people. It's not a shallow pond that dries up in times of drought. It's an endless ocean, not just for those who seem to have it all together.

For the longest time, I carried the belief that my weaknesses and

---

[44] Brennan Manning, *The Relentless Tenderness of Jesus* (Grand Rapids: Baker 2004), 24.

imperfections were a barrier to experiencing God's presence. I convinced myself that I had to fix my flaws and become more "suitable" before I could come near Him. But then, the waves of grief and trauma hit me, and I was left reeling with confusion and pain. In that darkness, I realized that my humanity did not surprise God. It's my vulnerability that made me approach Him!

Slowly, I began to understand that true humility is not about putting on a show of perfection but about coming to God in all my stumbling, messy, and broken reality. I didn't have to hide my weakness or pretend everything was okay. Instead, I could bare all my confusion, doubt, despair, and rebellion before Him.

And you know what? In doing so, I discovered that I was not a burden to God. He didn't see me as a mess but as His beloved child worthy of love and grace. With this realization came a deep sense of hope and resilience.

God's love is for everyone, especially those who fall into despair, depression, or doubt. It's for the ones who feel like they're drowning. It's for those of us who can barely keep our heads above water.

The more I embrace this truth, the more I find the courage to share my struggles with others to be vulnerable about my depression, anxiety, doubts, and failures. I want others to see me not as someone who has it all together but as someone swimming in this ocean of grace. During my journey, I have discovered that many others also struggle to stay afloat—those looking for a hand or a lifeboat. And I desire to be that hand for others.

So I keep swimming forward, even when the waves are high and the sky is dark, because I know the ocean of grace is more extensive than my fears or failures. And no matter how far I drift or how deep I sink, there is always a lifeguard on duty. We've been given a choice. We can either be broken by fear and shame or entirely made whole by His love.

I am still a work in progress, and I know I will always be. But now, I approach each day with renewed creativity and courage. No matter what challenges come my way, I can face them with vulnerability, honesty, and the knowledge that I am loved just as I am.

Finding and living out our most authentic selves is a lifelong journey. It is not something that happens overnight. There's no formula, three-step process, or checklist to unmasking your most authentic self. Instead, we must learn to listen to the still, small voice of the Holy Spirit and simply hold space for ourselves and others to feel. Our freedom is in Christ.

The moments when we are quiet and still before God awaken us to the reality of His love, revealing our most authentic selves: the person He created us to be.

When we make room to "be" and let go of our preconceived ideas of what this journey should look like, we step into a beautiful journey with Christ.

---

### DIGGING DEEPER:

1. Embrace your worth as a beloved child: Recognize that you are not a burden to God but a cherished and loved child. Allow this truth to shape your perspective and infuse you with hope and resilience.

2. How can you embrace the growth process? What steps do you need to take to help you understand that healing and personal growth are ongoing journeys? Remember, you are a work in progress, so approach each day with creativity and courage, knowing you can face challenges with vulnerability and honesty.

3. Feel all the feelings without guilt or shame: Allow yourself to experience and express various emotions. Release any guilt or shame associated with feeling and instead extend compassion to yourself and others. Take some time to journal your thoughts.

# CHAPTER 10

## UNBURDENED BY FORGIVENESS

*"Ultimately, mourning means facing what wounds us in the presence of one who can heal us."*[45]

On Christmas Eve, Douglas reopens the door of our private nightmare when he decides to pop those pills to once more numb the pain. He succumbs to the screaming lies that he is unworthy. On New Year's Eve, my husband drives him to another rehab. How, in the name of all things good and right, do we end up back here?

There's no way to avoid the pain. There is no way to avoid the brokenness.

Brokenness… it's not something we celebrate or invite into our lives.

No one wants to be broken and needy. It feels unnatural to come to the end of ourselves with nowhere to go but up.

Yet, this is what my family is: broken.

Mike and I sit in front of a computer screen, feeling the moment's

---

[45] Henri Nouwen, *Turn My Mourning Into Dancing: Finding Hope in Hard Times* (Nashville: Thomas Nelson, 2004).

weight. I want to break down, curl up on the floor, and bawl. Grasping the side of the table, we patiently wait for Douglas and his therapist to log on to the Zoom call. Small talk is made. All the weeks of Douglas being at this second rehab bleed into streams of the darkest nights.

Tenderly, I brace myself, knowing that the next hour will be challenging. We've known since Douglas's first therapy appointment this moment was coming. Mike, and I were required to write and read an impact letter to Douglas as part of his treatment, which is a letter stating how his drug use has affected the family and, most importantly, the knowledge that we all forgive him.

Not an easy task. Writing the letter reveals something I didn't know existed: unforgiveness for Douglas and myself. I hold myself responsible for the way Douglas's life turned out. I rake myself through the coals every time he makes a wrong choice. The magnifying glass I use to examine my every move as his mom points to all my failures. "You are never enough for him!" my mind screams. I'm not perfect, so of course, it's all my fault he's in rehab. Only "hurt people, hurt people," right? How did I fail to love him?

I didn't realize until I put pen to paper that my unforgiveness toward Douglas and myself puts a wedge in my relationship with him and God.

We often scratch our heads in disbelief because we feel stuck in our journey and don't know what's wrong with us. The complexity of emotions is nearly impossible to untangle, but maybe hiding under all the emotion is a tangled-up mess of past hurts and unforgiven wounds. Hurts from the one you lost or unforgiven wounds from the person who's inflicted such grief and turmoil. Maybe you've harbored unforgiveness toward yourself or perhaps even God. As a result, anger and bitterness can creep in without us even knowing it and rob us of the peace and joy God intended for us.

Forgiveness is hard.

It's a delicate and transformative act that beckons us to dig deep into the recesses of our souls. It's not a sign of weakness. It takes immense courage to release the grip of anger, resentment, and bitterness that can consume us. It is a conscious choice to break free from the chains of the past and embrace the liberating path of healing. It requires vulnerability, introspection, and a courageous willingness to confront the pain that lingers within. Though challenging, I've found that the journey of forgiveness holds the potential to unlock profound healing and liberation. I encourage you not to sink back but to press in.

Ultimately, forgiveness is an invitation from God to experience more of Him. Remember, we are in this together.

You are not alone. Not overlooked.

I wrestle with the burden of resentment and hurt in the depths of my heart. Yet, I couldn't seem to pioneer my feelings. Carrying the grudges toward myself and harboring bitterness toward Douglas consumes all my energy. The resentment and bitterness took a toll on my body.

In those moments of writing the letter, I realized forgiveness isn't about condoning the actions that wounded me but rather about freeing myself from the shackles of anger and resentment. It wasn't about the elaborate words...because sometimes, the only words we can utter are, "I need God to move. Help me to forgive."

The wounds of loved ones who have passed still exist, and maybe no reconciliation has ever taken place on this side of heaven. Forgiveness is for us, my friends, not them.

Unfortunately, feelings don't necessarily align with beliefs, so we get stuck. Feelings tell you it hurts and there's no way to forgive, while beliefs tell you to forgive and move on. You know, bite your tongue. Hold back your complaint.

Except there has to be a balance of the two. You cannot wrap up and tie forgiveness with a big red bow. You can't slap a bandaid on a weeping wound and pretend it's not there. Rather, it is an ongoing process requiring an open heart and a willingness to release the pain of the past and move forward with grace and strength.

It's a daily release.

Forgiveness is similar to a garden: the only way to cultivate a healthy and beautiful garden is to weed, prune, and care for it daily. You can't just plant the seeds and expect them to grow without time and effort. It takes ongoing care and attention to create a thriving garden. Forgiveness is not about the other person but about us and our spirit.

Although I know it's essential to process the hurt, I often sabotage it. Instead of cultivating heart responses that allow me to move forward, I halt the journey, beating down any hints of joy and peace that start to blossom. Sometimes, I feel powerless to change because of unexpected circumstances, but sometimes, it's because of my decisions and choices. And I don't want to live like that anymore.

As we embark on this journey of forgiveness, let us remember that growth is not linear. Some days will be more challenging, and setbacks will occur. But with each act of forgiveness, no matter how small, we plant seeds of hope and renewal within our hearts. We create a fertile ground for personal growth, emotional well-being, and the restoration of our relationships.

Forgiveness doesn't come by osmosis. It begins with brokenness. Forgiving those who hurt us is humbling, and it takes brokenness to admit that unforgiveness robs us of enjoying life in Christ.

In the intricate tapestry of life, our path is not always a straight line but a twisted journey leading us closer to the heartbeat of God. As a result, we try to avoid twists and turns in the wrong direction.

My heart questioned the purpose of the winding road when it seemed to lead further from our desired destination. I rehearsed angry words between Douglas and me. If only we could go back and do it all over again. If only I hadn't said those nasty things. If only he hadn't taken that first sip or had said no to the first hit. If only I had done more and somehow silenced my lies of unworthiness. *If only...* except there's no way back. We cannot undo the past.

But we can't focus on wanting to undo the past; we must focus on moving forward, always and forever, toward the God we love and the people we love. God can reconstruct our lives in the brokenness, creating something new and beautiful. The shattered dreams and perceived failures we experience can be transformed into masterpieces just as a broken dish can become a mosaic of possibilities!

There's beauty that arises from our mistakes and setbacks. Within the brokenness lies a hidden strength, a profound resilience, and a limitless capacity to rise and become more than we ever imagined.

Redemption is worth the fight.

In the intricate web of our human existence, it is not suffering that weighs heaviest upon our souls. Instead, it's the profound sense of isolation from the unforgiven inflicted emotional wounds we carry. The isolation we feel traces back to the days of Eden, when the bonds between humanity and God were fractured, leaving us wounded and vulnerable.

While suffering inflicts its wounds upon us, it is the *aftermath* of this suffering that genuinely shapes us. How we respond to suffering erodes our relationship with God and fractures the ties that bind us to one another. In the wake of hardship, we grapple with the consequences of broken trust, shattered attachments, and profound isolation.

Today, I see a glimmer of hope in moments of vulnerability. I recognize the most significant affliction is not the pain itself but how it chips away at my connections—with God and Douglas. This awareness empowers me to confront my deepest wounds and embrace healing and reconciliation.

The computer screen finally reveals Douglas and his therapist. Bravely, I look into my son's eyes, only to see the little boy I once held on my lap. I see greatness.

With trembling lips, I slowly read the letter:

"Dear Douglas,

We are writing you this letter because we love you and know you need help, and without help, your life and future are at stake. This letter is also to help support you in reaching your therapeutic goals to be healthy and whole. As we sit and write this letter, one thought pervades: "We had an amazing son: loving, caring, smart, creative, talented, graduated a year early, top of his class. Then addiction took the best of him."

Addiction took the best of him.

Then grief and trauma took the best of us.

Sitting in the wake of his choices, I immediately see that restoring our relationship is the key to breaking the chains of suffering. By acknowledging the impact of our brokenness, we can begin to rebuild the dismantled bridges. Through forgiveness, we are given a path toward redemption to mend our fractured bonds through vulnerability, introspection, and resilience.

In this revelation, I find peace and a renewed sense of purpose. Our collective struggle doesn't just consist of suffering but of restoring our relationships—with God, ourselves, and one another. We nurture those connections to reclaim our most authentic selves and journey toward wholeness.

As I continue to read with tears streaming down my face, something inside me breaks. All those times of withdrawing and turning inward, looking for anything to numb the pain, looking for a distraction from the hurt, there was a seed of unforgiveness toward Douglas and me.

I just want to embrace him.

All of this is so challenging. No one wants to face how suffering has broken something within their soul or, even worse, their relationships. Who wants to forgive in the face of unbelievable grief?

Exhaustion overtakes me.

I've done everything I know to do. I've poured out every need in helplessness and grief. There's freedom in dying to yourself and finding freedom through forgiveness as we come to God with a sense of bankruptcy, a desperate need for Him to move in our spirits. God will show up.

His Word says that this is our greatest sacrifice: *"The sacrifices to God are a broken spirit; a broken and contrite heart, O God you will not despise"* (Psalm 51:17).

The word "contrite" is defined as something crushed into small particles or ground into powder. Oh, I for sure felt broken into a million pieces. Throughout the breaking, the grief, and the forgiveness, God remade my will so that my identity could be based solely on Him. Christ bore His body on the cross not only for the forgiveness of sins but for my identity to be in Him!

Rather than focusing on outward appearances, God peers into our hearts. While we see broken relationships as something beyond repair and consider them unsalvageable, God sees them as a source of profound beauty and a valuable asset capable of mending. Victory comes when we see our insufficiency and acknowledge God to help us toward forgiveness. Then, our eyes turn from our lack to His great power. God's character and agenda are our primary focus.

You have to stay close to the Word to know the heartbeat of God.

Nehemiah, a figure of strength and resilience, demonstrated a remarkable response to God that encapsulates vulnerability and hope. With his heart heavy and burdened, Nehemiah recognized the brokenness of his people and the city. The walls of Jerusalem lay in ruins, a poignant reflection of the state of their community. Yet, instead of succumbing to despair, Nehemiah chose to turn his gaze toward God. Little did Nehemiah know God was about to take his desperate situation and turn it into a great miracle. In his response to God's promises, Nehemiah exemplified hope:

*"Remember the word that you commanded your servant Moses..."* (Nehemiah 1:8).

Nehemiah trusted that even in devastation, God's faithfulness would prevail. Nehemiah understood that true resilience emerges when we surrender our brokenness, allowing God to guide us through the arduous journey of rebuilding.

With a resilient spirit and unwavering faith, Nehemiah rallied his people and embarked on a transformative endeavor. Together, they faced countless obstacles, encountered resistance, and persevered in adversity to return to Jerusalem after seventy years in exile. Nehemiah's brokenness over losing his people's city became a beacon of hope for those around him. He demonstrated that greatness can emerge from the depths of despair.

*"Come, let's rebuild Jerusalem's wall so we will no longer be a disgrace"* (Nehemiah 2:17).

What can we glean from Nehemiah's wisdom?

First, Nehemiah acknowledged his need for God and completely trusted Him. Turn to God in your time of need and pour your heart before Him. If you find yourself in a place of restlessness and bitterness, not hearing from God, stay before Him. He will speak and give you directions.

In the face of immense suffering, Nehemiah prayed in brokenness and desperation, approaching God with a broken spirit, an attitude of humility and surrender. When he heard the devastating news of Jerusalem's walls broken and its gates destroyed, he wept, prayed, and fasted for days (Nehemiah 1:4).

Some days, I find myself babbling before God in a puddle of tears. I've already expressed all my hurts and disappointments to Him. Sure, it may not look like I am moving Heaven, but my God hears me, and peace floods my soul. Stay strong, my friend. Nehemiah prayed for *four months* before approaching Persia's king for help. God gave him great favor before the king and an incredible vision for the run-down city because Nehemiah waited on God! When Nehemiah waited on God, He moved Heaven and Earth to respond, providing him with favor before the king and a vision for his city. Even when it feels like we are not getting a response, God is listening and will answer us in His time.

When we acknowledge our need for God and trust Him, we will see new possibilities in our seemingly impossible tasks. For example, Nehemiah could experience the power of God's favor and see the extraordinary results of an almost impossible task by waiting on God. So, likewise, if we trust Him, we can expect the same!

Second, Nehemiah repented.

In his brokenness, Nehemiah found an unshakable strength. He didn't shy away from the pain or attempt to hide his emotions. Instead, he allowed his spirit to be vulnerable before God, acknowledging his sins and the sins of his people: *"...I now pray before you day and night for the people of Israel, your servants, confessing the sins of the people of Israel, which we have sinned against you. Even I and my father's house have sinned"* (Nehemiah 1:6).

Never underestimate the need to repent. Repenting is a courageous act of taking responsibility for sins, acknowledging shortcomings, and turning away from them. In this act of repentance, we depend on God's boundless grace. After we repent, we can turn from sin and rely on His grace. Repentance opens the door to transformation. Taking responsibility for our sins and turning away from them allows God's grace to give us the strength to walk in righteousness. As we humbly accept God's grace, we enter into a transformative relationship with Him and others, allowing us to experience the hope and joy of living a life that reflects His perfect will.

As a result of his repentance, Nehemiah discovered a wellspring of resilience in this space of brokenness, which fueled his determination to rebuild and restore.

Nehemiah's broken spirit became a catalyst for change. It sparked creative energy, driving him to envision a better future for God's people. He sought wisdom through prayer and by remembering who God is, drawing strength from God's promises and wisdom.

In the intricacies of our faith journey, sacrifices are not enough to please the Lord. The state of our spirit, heart, sincerity, and the authenticity of our repentance truly resonates with the Lord. In the humility of our confession and the depth of our forgiveness, our spirits become receptive vessels, ready to receive abundant life from the Spirit.

In the early hours of the morning of that Zoom call, the Lord whispered to my heart, urging me to embrace the transformative power of a second layer of forgiveness toward Douglas.

Forgiveness is not a one-time thing. It's a daily practice of acknowledging imperfections, embracing humanity, and extending grace. In the sacred space of vulnerability, I discovered the transformative power of forgiveness.

My dear friend, forgiveness is not merely a one-time event but a courageous and transformative daily act. It requires us to delve deep within ourselves, peeling back the layers of hurt and resentment accumulated over time. It is an introspective journey that demands vulnerability, introspection, and unwavering faith.

Finally, Nehemiah reminded God of His promises.

We declare God's promises, not because He forgets to honor them, but because we ignore them. *"Remember the word that you commanded your servant Moses…"* (Nehemiah 1:8). When we remind God of His word, we tap into the timeless wisdom and unchanging love that flows. We declare our belief in the faithfulness of His promises, knowing that His word never returns void. Our spirits will gain courage in these moments of remembrance, and our resilience will fortify.

God desires us to live utterly dependent on Him. Utter dependence ensures the abundant life we so desperately long for.

I can assure you, friend, that He will meet you in your darkest moments and overtake you with His peace. His presence will sustain you. His promise to never leave you or forsake you is accurate. He is the steady Rock in this unshakable world.

Nehemiah wept. Fasted and prayed. Nehemiah became a great leader who led the Israelite nation to rebuild the city walls.

So, what is on the other side of your brokenness?

When we let our guard down and stop pretending we have it all together, God moves and takes great delight in us. Brokenness is not a feeling or emotion but part of our will.

All God wants is our hearts, no matter how broken and wounded they are. The fact that God loves me and accepts me just as I am has been difficult to understand until I forgave my earthly father for his faults. I always felt like I had to earn God's love and acceptance, just like I did with my dad's. Despite my efforts to do more, it never felt like it was enough.

For most of my childhood, my dad wasn't around. Not because he didn't want to be, but because he thought providing financially for our family was best. I needed him when I hit my teens, and he wasn't there. My attempts to find love and acceptance from the wrong places resulted in new wounds. These wounds carried not only into my marriage but also into my relationship with God. I began serving a god who demanded of me rather than loved me. Never being able to live up to those expectations left a void for acceptance that I was eager to fill.

It wasn't until I hit my thirties that the Holy Spirit began a work of forgiveness toward my dad. I learned to function as a daughter whom the King loved. I no longer needed acceptance from others and could love my earthly dad fully by choosing to let go of all the hurt and pain.

There was no magic cure for the lack of a relationship with my dad over the last thirty years. My father never even uttered the words, "Will you forgive me?" Throughout the years, I have heard many people say, "I'm sorry" without changing. Words without action have no meaning. I've learned that there doesn't have to be anything formal said to forgive those who have hurt you.

Because real forgiveness comes from God, *He* provides it! In her book *Unashamed*, Christine Caine says, "Sure, we try to love, but love from a broken heart is broken love. Love from a wounded soul is wounded love. Love from a tormented mind is tormented love. And this affects not only how we love God but how we love ourselves and our neighbors. As long as shame has a grip on our lives, to put it bluntly, our love is messy."[46] Without God, we can't love or forgive others correctly. No one can give what they don't have.

Forgiveness isn't overlooking the wrong or letting the injustice go unpunished. Denial only places a bandaid on the wound. A wound won't heal just because you pretend it didn't happen. A forgiving attitude isn't about ignoring the wound but looking squarely at the offense and seeing it in its true light. C.S. Lewis wrote, "Real forgiveness means looking steadily at the sin, the sin that is left over without any excuse, after all, allowances have been made, and seeing it in all its horror, dirt, meanness and malice, and nevertheless being wholly reconciled to the (person) who has done it."[47] Not easy, huh?

A new connection between my dad and I emerged before he became ill. Small conversations. I spent weeks at my parent's house with the kids. Dad spent time fishing with my boys. Presence. It all weaved together,

---

[46] Christine Caine, *Unashamed: Drop the Baggage, Pick Up Your Freedom, Fulfill Your Destiny* (Nashville: Thomas Nelson, 2016).

[47] *The Weight of Glory: And Other Addresses.* HarperOne 2001.

forming a new relationship.

And it was good.

I never expected God to redeem the time and allow special moments while my dad was sick. After years of never hearing "I love you," I often heard it with kisses on my hand as I sat by his bedside.

Redemption is possible for any relationship. *Never* think that any situation is too far gone for our God! Keep believing and forgive!

Forgiveness is not about them. It's for you and God!

When my dad died, I was deeply grateful for our time together, and I knew he loved me in his own way.

Regarding Douglas, my forgiveness looked different. It's ongoing. I began to forgive him, and I still have to extend forgiveness to him repeatedly. In Matthew 18, Peter asks Jesus, *"How many times shall I forgive my brother when he sins against me? Up to seven times?" Jesus answered, "I tell you, you must forgive him more than seven times. You must forgive him even if he wrongs you seventy times seven"* (Mathew 18:22).

This truth plays out with all my relationships. Even the relationship with myself! And even sometimes God. It may sound counter-intuitive because God is *God* and doesn't do anything wrong. But sometimes, you may feel like He could have done something to stop the suffering and make it all better.

If forgiveness doesn't become a daily habit, you will drag last week's hurts into today's arguments. It will compound, hurt upon hurt, wound upon a wound. And I get it. We feel the need to hold on to the pain and hurt because we want to control the punishment others, and even ourselves, receive. But this mindset becomes a snowball rolling down a hill, getting bigger and bigger with each roll until it's a massive boulder that's almost impossible to stop. Forgiveness is the key to breaking that cycle before it gets out of control.

With Douglas, forgiveness looks like letting go of resentment and bitterness over and over again. Forgiveness has become my life preserver in the waves of trauma and grief. I'm slowly embracing the unexpected turns with hope and resilience, finding peace even in uncertainty. I have been shaped and molded into my most authentic self. The winding road became a sacred pilgrimage, inviting me to trust the process and surrender to the plan unfolding before me.

Forgiveness is an act of surrender. We can't control or change the outcome after we forgive, and we certainly don't have all the answers. The best thing we can do is trust in God's greater plan. Through surrendering to the journey God has ordained for us, we can find peace by understanding that forgiveness. This is the ultimate act of letting go and trusting God.

## DIGGING DEEPER:

Ponder this verse: *"So (instead of further rebuke, now) you should turn and (graciously) forgive and comfort and encourage (her/him) to keep (her/him) from being overwhelmed by excessive sorrow and despair."*[48]

1. Are you carrying any unforgiveness? Toward yourself or others? Maybe it's toward someone you lost, and reconciliation is not an option. Remember, forgiving the other person is for your healing.

2. If you struggle to forgive someone, talk to God about it. Maybe even write a letter to the person expressing your feelings, and remember you don't necessarily have to give it to the person; forgiveness is for your healing.

---

[48] 2 Corinthians 2:7 AMP

# CHAPTER 11

## EMBRACING THE RELEASE

*"The holes in our lives can become places of hope."*[49]

Douglas returns from the out-of-state rehab right before his eighteenth birthday, and then a week later, I discover his room empty one morning. He's gone again. This last rehab had been an extended care program where eight men lived in a house, doing daily life together—a six-month program designed to help people with addiction learn how to live sober daily. Douglas hated it and called daily, begging us to let him come home. He made many empty promises to us—promises of getting a job and attending meetings if we let him come home and mending his relationship with us, especially with his sister. Lie after lie about how awful the people were there at the rehab. Of course, he thought he would do better at home. Eventually, he wore us down, and against his counselor's advice, we signed him out a week before his birthday.

Do I regret that decision? I don't know. Douglas isn't ready to be sober, and we've exhausted our resources and ourselves. Honestly, we have nothing left to give.

As I walk into Douglas's room, realizing he's gone, I feel a familiar

---

[49] Lana Bateman, prayer advocate for Women of Faith, in prayer offered at Harford, CT, event on November 3, 2012.

THE FREEDOM TO FEEL

wave of grief washing over me. Disoriented at first. Is he really gone?

An array of emotions flood in, catching me off guard. Unable to harness them, I collapse onto his bed; the weight of the grief becomes palpable, permeating every fiber of my being. It's like discovering my dad's brain tumor all over again. Taking my breath away, I feel like a heavy anchor has fallen onto my heart.

Grief isn't logical, and it's certainly not predictable. I try to brace myself against the overwhelming sorrow. All my emotions pour out in a cascade of tears and sobs, releasing the pent-up emotions I held captive for the last few days, watching Douglas struggle. One of the difficult aspects of grief is how it resurfaces, sometimes unexpectedly, like waves crashing upon the shore. When you think you've found your footing, grief hits you, reminding you that it's still there, waiting to be acknowledged and processed.

I'd later discover this complicated dance of grief and trauma is associated with cumulative loss. It's when one loss rolls into another without fully grieving the first. The accumulated pain may return with the current pain. It's like a weight growing heavier with each passing moment. Each sorrowful event marks our journey. It can be overwhelming.

My life is like a cascading domino effect, one tragic event leading to another, each toppling into the next in a seemingly never-ending cycle. First, my dad died of a rare brain tumor. Then, eleven months later, my mom was diagnosed with a rare type of uterine cancer. Next, COVID wreaked havoc on our lives, and just when we were catching our breath from being quarantined, our house burned to the ground. Then, six months later, Douglas began to spiral into his addiction and the long month of being in the hospital with my other son.

Cumulative loss is not a linear path but a complex tapestry of intertwined emotions that begin to shatter pieces of our hearts we never knew were even there. Each loss leaves its mark, like a thread unraveling from the fabric of our lives. It becomes a collection of broken dreams, shattered hopes, and the ache of what could have been. As these losses accumulate, we may grapple with the immense weight of grief, struggling to understand it all.

The diagnosis.

The prognosis.

The anxiety.

The questions.

The unknowns.

The bills are piling high.

The job loss.

The empty crib.

The death of a loved one.

However, these accumulated losses invite us to the transformative power of letting go and embracing new paths. In her book *Healing through the Dark Emotions, Miriam Greenspan* beautifully captures this essence as she speaks of grief's gifts and ability to unveil a deeper understanding of life's intricate tapestry. She calls this the "alchemy of grief," meaning its transformative power and invitation to let go of old ways of being and grow into new ways. "The gift that grief offers us," Greenspan writes, "is the capacity to deeply see how things are. Life is limited. We are here for a short time. Grief asks us to know this, not only in a disembodied, cerebral way but in the marrow of our bones—to look into the reality of death and loss without our usual egoic blinders on."[50]

Processing grief requires deep introspection that will teach us many lessons. It shapes us from within if we dare to listen to its whispers and feel its weight. In grief, we'll unearth the treasures within the depths of suffering. Grief finds its voice as we surrender to the emotions.

As I lie on Douglas's bed, I close my eyes, feeling a sense of relief as the wave of emotions pass, giving me the strength to face reality. There is a new sense of peace, clarity, and acceptance. I take a deep breath, listening to the silence. Accepting the silence allows me to move forward.

---

[50] Miriam Greenspan, *Healing Through the Dark Emotions: The Wisdom of Grief, Fear, and Despair* (United Kingdom: Shambhala, 2004), 103.

I ask myself, though every fiber of my being feels worn out: "Is there anything else I need to grieve?" The Word of God gives me direction, *"I cried out to the Lord in my suffering, and he heard me"* (Psalm 34:6).

C.S. Lewis once wrote, "We can ignore... our pleasure. But our pain insists upon being attended to. God whispers to us in our pleasures, speaks in our conscience, but shouts in our pain: It is His megaphone to rouse a deaf world."[51]

I texted a friend the following day, "The pain of losing Douglas again is almost too much to bear."

The protective shield of shock and numbness fades, and the raw reality sets in. Suddenly, instead of standing on a firm foundation, I'm standing in quicksand, and no matter how hard it is to move, I continue trying and trying. And I wonder if I'd ever find the firm ground beneath my feet again.

Someone once described losing a loved one "like having a tree that has been growing in one's heart yanked out by its roots, leaving a gaping hole or wound."

As a mother, I often ponder my kids' journeys into adulthood. There's a call for youth to leave the safe havens of their family and venture into the unknown with no guarantee they'll succeed like we thought.

When my son left, embarking on his own journey, I felt a deep sense of loss instead of joy in anticipating his future. His departure seems more like a death than a launch into manhood. I surrender my fears and let him go, trusting he will find his way back to the course intended for him. His journey will have its challenges, but he is learning the lessons needed to become the man God intended him to be. I pray he'll soon see the light that shines in the darkness and find wisdom and purpose in life.

In hindsight of that fateful day, I can now see that Douglas wanted to conquer his hero's journey. He's always been one to figure out life independently; this situation was no different. He wants to do everything on his own. So, his only choice was to leave home and venture into the

---

[51] Bruce L. Davis, "The Atheistic Problem of Good," *Atheistic Problem of Good* (thesis, 2023), https://core.ac.uk/download/568250612.pdf.

unknown to overcome his addiction, learning how to live sober without his parents' help.

Letting him go is like a balloon slowly slipping away, releasing my grip on the string and eventually losing it in the vast expanse of the sky. I watch in disappointment and sadness as he drifts further away. Loss can feel like that, sometimes. It's complex and uncertain, with a knotted-up mess of emotions. It's like letting go of that balloon string and having it get tangled with a bunch of uncertainty and fear.

Fully embracing grief is daunting. It's as if surrendering to its depths means being forever engulfed by its relentless tide. I don't want to feel this deep pain anymore.

It's natural to hesitate, to question whether allowing ourselves to feel will only perpetuate our suffering.

In this entanglement, there lies a paradox. By accepting the reality of our losses and allowing ourselves to grieve, we find the potential for healing and growth. We must release our grip on what once was, even though it feels like a piece of ourselves is slipping away. There's no question that the pain is undeniable, and life as you knew it is gone.

Just like it's painful when a doctor sets a broken bone for healing, it's emotionally painful to take steps forward bravely and face the ache head-on.

Grieving forces us to see the reality of the finality of our loss and accept the irrevocable changes it entails. It means letting go of what I expected Douglas's life to look like.

Letting go can feel like an amputation, like part of our identity is severed.

Experiencing my shortcomings as a mom is an unpredictable kind of grief. Yet, within this acceptance of imperfection, an unexpected wellspring of resilience arises.

How can I navigate the challenges of life without knowing where Douglas is?

As we eat dinner that evening, we all feel the weight of his absence. He'd been gone before, but this feels different. It felt final. Despite the pain of failure and the emptiness of his seat at our table, I unearth a new strength to confront my fears and keep going. Even though I still don't know when I'll see him again, I choose to live in the present moment and savor the little things.

Grief symbolizes love and connection, conveying how our loss profoundly impacts our lives. It's acknowledging the void left behind, recognizing that life will never be the same. But even within this recognition, there is always hope. In facing our grief, we honor what was lost, find the strength to release, and move forward, discovering reservoirs of strength we never knew existed. We gather the shattered fragments of our lives, knowing that they carry the weight of our losses and the potential for growth and renewal. We learn to hold space for pain and healing, acknowledging that both can coexist.

I continue embracing the knotted-up mess of emotions one day at a time, understanding that it's all an integral part of the journey.

We don't hear from Douglas much since he's currently homeless and without a phone. I cradle my much-needed coffee cup, inhaling and exhaling slowly. My heart's breaking from the weariness of the past week. At unexpected times, waves of sadness crash against my worn-out soul. Abby struggles with anxiety, Douglas is gone, and the building of our new house is fraught with difficulties.

I ache for my old life, before the fire, before Douglas fell into addiction, before the grief and pain. I longed for those days to return to the place where I felt carefree.

Every day takes courage. Facing the reality of my circumstances and not pretending I'm okay took me from knowing God to *needing* God.

Choosing to feel all the emotions led to healing and acceptance of our current life.

But it's hard. I'm still not there yet.

I get lost in the cycle of questioning and doubts, trying to make sense of the suffering. Deep in the tangled-up mess of emotions, questions emerge again and again. "Why is this happening? Why has God allowed Douglas to spiral again? Is everything going to be okay?"

I'm angry. Angry at God for allowing this to happen. Angry that our family seems to be the only ones suffering, Angry at Douglas for not trying harder to fight the addiction. His leaving caused so much pain not only for Mike and me but for his siblings, too.

Grabbing my pen, I wrote, "Today I feel angry..." in my journal, and for the next few minutes, I got *real* honest with God.

Raw honesty before God becomes the fertile ground where seeds of change are sown.

I sigh as I copy a verse from Psalms. Writing the psalm word is the best way for me to grasp its power. *"Why, O Lord, do you stand far off? Why do you hide yourself in times of trouble?"* (Psalm 10:1).

Job asked "why" sixteen times, and it never upset God. It's natural to feel overwhelmed and ask "why" in moments of struggle. It's not a sign of weakness but rather a reflection of the depth of our emotions.

As humans, we're wired to ask "why." As children, we ask this question with wide-eyed wonder and boundless curiosity. But, as we grow older, we become entrenched in the rational and reasonable approaches that society values. We rely on our tools and vices to control and explain the mysterious workings of God. But what if asking "why" is necessary to process and release difficult emotions?

What if asking "why" is more than just a question? What if it's a vulnerable cry from the heart, a way of expressing that things aren't as they should be?

In asking, we acknowledge life's complexity; sometimes, things happen we can't fully comprehend. Asking "why" is a desperate cry for *meaning* amidst the chaos. It causes us to grapple with unfair circumstances, seek answers, and allow ourselves to process and make sense of our pain.

Even when no answers come, asking keeps us vulnerable and reflective. In the asking, we confront our emotions, doubts, and uncertainties and release the grip of suffering on our hearts and minds.

Sometimes, the enemy pushes us further into the dark, making us believe we have no business seeking answers. But God promises, *"I will lead you beside still waters. I will restore your soul"* (Psalm 23:2-3).

Moving forward in grief does not start when we simply stop asking "why" or strive to stop feeling pain. Instead, among the questioning, suffering becomes a part of our story, and rather than hanging onto bitterness and control, we step into God's plans for moving forward. In the process, we express ourselves honestly and openly—allowing our vulnerable cries from the heart to be heard.

Just like Job, we can turn our questions into an opportunity to deepen our understanding and intimacy with God. It's okay to feel the weight of sadness and disappointment, but we must hold onto the belief that there is more beyond the pain.

In his deep anguish and despair, Job poses heartfelt questions to God, seeking understanding and a sense of justice: "Why didn't I die at birth, my first breath of the womb my last? I could be resting in peace right now, asleep forever, feeling no pain..."[52]

In response, God reveals Himself in a powerful and transformative way.

*"Where were you when I laid the foundations of the earth?"* (Job 38:4). *"Have you ever in your days commanded the morning light?"* (Job 38:12). *"Where does light live, or where does darkness reside?"* (Job 38:19). *"Can you lead out a constellation in its season?"* (Job 38:32).

Of course, the correct response to all of these questions is, "No, I don't command the universe! I don't know the answers!" But, instead of trying to find answers, Job was humbled by the power of God's majesty. He could not begin to comprehend the depths of the universe, and he admitted that he could not harness or control its power.

God's answer to Job's questions is not a direct explanation nor a simple resolution to his suffering. Instead, God's response takes the form

---

[52] Job 3:11-12 MSG.

of a series of rhetorical questions and reflections on the vastness and complexity of creation. God invites Job to contemplate the wonders of the natural world, the mysteries of the universe, and the sovereignty of His wisdom and power.

Through this encounter, God reveals His unfathomable wisdom and reminds Job of the limitations of human understanding. God's response humbles Job and brings him to a place of awe and reverence. He invites Job to trust in divine providence and embrace a perspective that surpasses his immediate suffering.

God's answer to Job is a revelation of His grandeur and sovereignty. It reminds Job—and all of us—that we are part of a much larger story, intricately woven by a loving and all-knowing Creator. God's response to Job's questions teaches us that we may not always receive the answers in the face of suffering. However, God invites us to trust and rest in the assurance of His presence.

I wrote *"trust"* in my journal and then sat back, staring at the page. Fighting back tears, I knew the Lord was asking me to release my clenched fists around the need to know all the answers. Fear grips my heart, but simultaneously, the Father says, "Trust me. I love you."

Can I trust God with my son? Can I trust Him with my future? Can I trust that one day, He'll make all things new?

I can't help but think of the story of Abraham and Isaac in Genesis 22. Was God asking me to lay my son on the altar?

God beckoned Abraham to a sacred task in the quiet space between heaven and earth—to lay his beloved son, Isaac, upon the altar. This wasn't just any son; he was the embodiment of all God's covenant promises, the long-awaited fulfillment of Abram and Sarah's patient hope. Picture a quarter-century of waiting, Sarah's laughter echoing in the background, as time seemed to mock the possibility of a child. Yet, in improbable odds, God unfolded a divine drama. Sarah and Abraham's faith was ultimately tested.

We often think Abraham made this trek up the mountain in a few hours, but it was over three days. That's three days of holding the tension between what God asked him to do and hope for the future. I'm sure he had restless nights, not knowing if God would come through, and long days of thinking, "What if God doesn't save Isaac?" Yet, in Abraham's unwavering obedience, he demonstrated a profound trust in God's plan, even when it seemed incomprehensible.

As Abraham embarked on that journey up the mountaintop, his heart must have been heavy with many emotions.

And in his darkest moments, he probably asked, "Am I being punished? Why, God?"

Did Abraham wonder how he would comfort Sarah if he didn't come home with Isaac? How would their life continue with their son?

With each step up the mountain, I imagine the heaviness of the present moment overtook his breath. His face languished with concern and doubt when he had to answer Isaac's question, *"Where is the lamb for a burnt offering?"*

Perhaps Abraham contemplated all Sarah had hoped for over the last few years, reexamining their steps and rehearsing everything they said. Had they done something wrong?

I believe, at its heart, this story has significant prophetic meaning. It's a story about a man setting down his twenty-five-year-old dream, everything he's ever wanted, and surrendering it to God, trusting that his loving Father knows best, that God would provide something better (just as the writer of Hebrews notes in Hebrews 11:40).

In Abraham's vulnerability, I'm sure he questioned and wrestled. Yet, he chose to submit, knowing there was a higher purpose beyond his human comprehension.

As readers, we know the story from beginning to end, but Abraham didn't. He didn't know God would provide a different sacrifice.

In Abraham's story, we find a reflection of our own story. Our unexpected circumstances can test our resolve, and it can be tempting to succumb to despair or lose sight of the possibilities for healing and transformation. But Abraham's tale teaches us the power of holding onto that tension and embracing our reality with hope. As a result of this, Abraham could continue walking in uncertainty and pain.

In the tension between Abraham's love for his son and his devotion to God, we witness a powerful lesson about the transformative nature of surrender. As Abraham raised the knife, fully prepared to offer his son as a sacrifice, he revealed a level of faith and surrender that's hard to comprehend.

Despite the pain, struggle, and brokenness surrounding him, Abraham dared to confront the harsh realities of life head-on without looking the other way. Abraham's story reminds us that healing is not always immediate or accessible. Instead, through patience, perseverance, and an unwavering belief in the possibility of restoration, we experience the grace to endure—forging our strength between our present reality and our hope for healing.

Just as Abraham's hand poised to carry out the unthinkable, God intervened, saying, *"Abraham, Abraham!' And [Abraham] said, 'Here I am'"* (Genesis 22:11).

I don't understand why the waves of suffering keep pounding my life. Still, I know God will keep calling my name in my weakest moments, providing just what I need.

God provided a ram caught in the thicket, which spared Isaac's life, which is the overwhelming grace that showcases God's faithfulness. It spotlights Christ meeting us in our weakness and sustaining us in sorrow.

There's a profound revelation in intertwining Abraham's trust and God's intervention. Laying Isaac on the altar was not merely a test of Abraham's obedience but a symbol of surrender—a willingness to release the most cherished dreams and desires into the hands of a loving and sovereign God.

Suffering asks us to bear under what is ultimately not our control, bullying us into surrendering control. Here, I'm facing a moment requiring a similar surrender to Abraham—a letting go of plans, expectations, and the certainty that life will be *"normal"* again regarding my son. In those moments, there's an invitation to lay my own Isaac on the altar, entrusting him to my heavenly Father's divine wisdom and providence.

Surrender displays the transformative power of God's grace through

147

suffering. Grace isn't just the power to overcome; it's the power to endure, to live in the tension.

We grow weary when we forget we are a people waiting in expectation, holding this tension. Christ has already conquered our suffering, and He will make everything new. We await His return.

Suffering is not the end of our story.

*"So Abraham called the name of that place, 'The Lord will Provide'"* (Genesis 22:12).

I marked this moment in my journal as "The Lord will Provide."

May we embrace the truth that in our acts of surrender, God reveals Himself in ways we cannot comprehend.

I don't think there's any other way forward *but* to surrender. Despite the difficulty, God's faithfulness and provision exceed my family's expectations.

Close your eyes briefly, taking in the reality that God is real and present with you.

Kneeling on the wood floor of our rental home, tears flowing, I pray for the grace to surrender Douglas to God–the lament, the grieving, and the surrendering combine as I pray before a God who loves me. And for one split second, I wonder if this is how Jesus felt, crying in the garden before His Father. *"My Father, if possible, may this cup be taken from me. Yet not as I will, but as you will"* (Matthew 26:39).

Jesus, fully man, fully God, lived between two worlds: what He wanted and what His father wanted. Two sides of prayer. Jesus revealed his humanity in this moment as He prayed a prayer of surrender.

"God, I believe you can perform a miracle, but I let go of the resentment if you don't answer how I expect. I release the fear of life not turning out like I thought."

It's a delicate dance of living fully present in both joy and sorrow; it is a courageous act to open our hearts to the kaleidoscope of emotions, refusing to let pain eclipse the joy in life.

Letting go reveals a deeper intimacy with God, a profound peace that surpasses understanding, and a renewed sense of purpose on our faith journey. We find comfort in that space of tension, knowing we are not alone. The Holy Spirit walks alongside us, offering comfort, guidance, and the promise of a future where wounds mend and hearts are made whole.

Even though Douglas may not be able to break his addiction on this side of heaven, I have faith that God will give our family the strength to keep going—one step at a time. I scoop up all my hurts to give to the only One who can heal. Once again, I ask Him to take the pain and use it for His glory because He can use it all, even the flawed, messed-up parts. I suddenly remember the Scripture I read the night before: *"You're blessed when you're at the end of your rope. With less of you, there is more of God and his rule."* [53]

As we continue to walk through grief and trauma, we will discover the power of grace, giving us resilience. It is the strength to carry the weight of our sorrow, the determination to rise each day, and the unwavering belief that we can find meaning and purpose beyond the pain. This grace gives us the willingness to walk beside others carrying their Isaacs.

His grace strengthens us to stand alongside others in pain and uncertainty. Grace carries us forward, even when our steps are heavy and our hearts ache. Grace gives us the resilience to guide us through the darkest hours. This quiet strength keeps us going, even when it feels impossible.

By His grace, we can rise from the depths and find light in the darkness. This grace reminds us that we can transform our pain into purpose and honor our losses by living meaningfully and authentically.

Grace gives us the strength to continue, even when our steps are heavy and our hearts ache.

So, let us hold the tension of honoring the pain while nurturing the hope for healing. We embrace vulnerability and resilience, knowing that within this delicate balance lies the transformative power to navigate life's

---

[53] Matthew 5:3, MSG

trials and emerge stronger on the other side.

It's an intricate dance—feeling the pain and discovering what lies ahead. It's a daily surrender, sometimes minute by minute.

Once I surrendered, I noticed a shift in my questioning from "Why me?" to "Why not me?" Instead of dwelling on the hardships and challenges, I started recognizing that suffering is an inevitable part of being human.

Why not me?

Suffering touches every one of us! Unfortunately, a lie has crept into our church culture, telling us that saying yes to Jesus means no to suffering in our lives.

But how will we experience God's sustaining grace if we never need it to walk through anything hard?

Let's begin by asking: "Why not me?"

In the Bible, the apostle Paul writes how he wants to know Christ and the power of His resurrection. There's no mention of him asking, "Why me?" when faced with hardship; rather, he embraces it as an opportunity to draw closer to God.

Our greatest gift is more of Jesus...and we experience that in suffering.

The following day, my eyes opened to the thought, "Douglas is still gone." Pulling myself out of bed, I wash my face and hear the door slam. I put down the washcloth and walk through the hall and out the door. I see Douglas walking up from the end of the steep hill of our driveway. He's been gone for days. His head is hung low in shame.

My husband walks quickly down the driveway to embrace him. No anger. No disappointment. A gentle embrace between father and son.

I try to breathe, knowing that he can't fight the demons that torment his mind. I don't understand why Douglas struggles to be loved, but

I know this to be true: just as my husband embraces my son, God is running to embrace us, too. Douglas hugs me, and I know he can feel my love without words.

After trauma, accepting the fact that you're loved sometimes takes time. It takes recognizing the randomness of life rather than blaming your actions and choices on what happened.

It's similar to accepting the cycle of the seasons—knowing that sometimes there will be cold and dark winter days but also knowing that the warmth and brightness of summer will inevitably arrive. Accepting and embracing the seasons of life can bring a sense of peace and calm. The elusive answer to "why" becomes clear—life is woven with beauty and tragedy.

Forgiveness and grace are not always a sudden revelation but a gradual unfolding. It is a patient dance, with delicate brush strokes on the canvas of our souls. In the gentle whispers of our hearts, we can hear God's voice guiding us. Some of the most beautiful stories of redemption happened because of deep brokenness.

Maybe one day, Douglas will feel the love and acceptance of His Father!

## DIGGING DEEPER:

1. How have your doubts and questions about faith led you to a deeper connection with God?

2. Can you recall when acceptance settled within your soul, even if it took time to arrive fully? How did it impact your perspective on suffering and life's unfolding journey?

3. In what ways do you hear God's gentle whispers guiding you on this journey? How do you cultivate a receptive heart to listen and discern His voice?

# PART 3

## CULTIVATING
## A SOUL RESPONSE

# CHAPTER 12

## UNLIKELY HOPE IN DESPAIR

*I will refresh the weary and satisfy the faint. (Jeremiah 31:25)*

Sadly, my dear friend Rachel's husband recently received a diagnosis of stage four cancer. Of course, nobody expects a diagnosis like that at only forty years old. In the face of a tumor that threatens her husband's body and their whole life, she has to shift into caregiving mode for her sick husband and three small children.

My heart hurts for her.

Over the past few years, I have seen cancer invade Rachel's mom's body, eventually resulting in the death of her mother. Now, cancer is attacking her husband's body. I've seen Rachel grieve and pull herself up from despair. Losing a mother is especially difficult when you are in your thirties and have children. The grief and sadness of her losses run deep, and the exhaustion of enduring wave after wave of sorrow is all too familiar. However, God's presence has been the source of her strength.

I'm heavy with grief.

It's not fair.

It seems cruel for one person to walk through one trauma after another. Sadness seeps into my bones, and the weariness a nap will never fix overwhelms me. Even though I cannot fully understand her suffering, I still feel her pain. My friend endures the uncertainty of what tomorrow holds.

This past week, she sat in a hospital room exhausted, unable to sleep, watching her 5-year-old son lay in bed, finally getting some rest.

After several ER visits, a middle-of-the-night ambulance ride, and thirty-plus hours later, her son finally found himself in the hospital with a rare skin condition that caused his skin to peel off, exposing vast areas of flesh and nerves.

Luckily, the morphine relieved some of his pain, and her mind slowly began to work through the events.

She certainly felt at the end of her rope and knew it. Just ten months earlier, Rachel's mom passed from ovarian cancer. Her mom, her biggest fan, confidant, supporter, and the best grandmother, died, causing grief to ravish my friend's body. Then, only five months after her mom's death, Rachel's husband received a diagnosis of a rare stage 4 neuroendocrine cancer, leaving her with fear and uncertainty on top of three kids to care for and virtually alone.

Now, with her son in the hospital, she felt helpless to ease his suffering.

People often describe her with three words: "the strong one." That, along with phrases such as "I don't know how she does it," "She does it with such courage," or even "I can't even imagine how she feels."

With these simple phrases, she knew others didn't understand. They had no idea what a day in her shoes looked like, and her loneliness only exacerbated her grief, making her feel like she couldn't ask for help.

Rachel often says, "I don't know how I do it either. I don't feel strong, but I *have* to be strong because that's what people expect of me. I feel like I can't share the truth with them because the truth is weakness, and I don't want them to see me as weak."

It's uncomfortable for others to imagine the reality that Rachel herself can't escape. They look at her and see courage because she's endured hell. They didn't see the losses she had endured or the brutal reality of caregiving.

After the grueling days in the hospital with her son, Rachel and I sat over coffee as she told me, "Caregiving is one of the most challenging things. It's emotionally draining, time-consuming, and lonely. Everyone wants to help, but most don't know how. Their platitudes are meant to ease the suffering but have the opposite effect. Instead, I feel as if I always have to be on, not show the hard stuff, the pain, the resentment, the worry and fear, the anger and exhaustion. So I paste on a smile and kept going because they thought I'm strong, so I had to be. But because they can't grasp the pain, I feel alone."

We all yearn to be known, understood, and truly seen. Regrettably, authentic empathy appears elusive for many. Witnessing others in pain, especially in ways you never knew could hurt, and feeling helpless in being unable to fix or alleviate it can be overwhelming. However, I want to convey that hope begins to stir when you acknowledge and honor the pain.

She continued to say, "I lost all pretense in that hospital room, finally realizing that I'm *not* strong enough and *can't* outmuscle the pain anymore. If I don't give myself space to feel, it will consume me and suffocate any life I have left. So, moving forward, I'm choosing vulnerability in learning to reach out and share the reality of my struggles."

Nothing magical happened in those moments. Not with fairy dust, anyway. However, something miraculous transpired—her eyes opened. In finally acknowledging the hardness of her season and opening up about its reality, chains broke off the chambers of her soul.

In this season of grief and suffering, God revealed that if we don't allow others in and allow ourselves to feel, the unfelt pain will stake its territory in the hidden corners of our minds and hearts, and it will own us.

When someone asks, "Are you okay?" she honestly says, "I'm not, and here's what's hard right now." She's also writing and opening up about her grief and loss on social media and in person, giving a window for whoever is willing to show up authentically.

Amazingly, God designed us to heal within relationships. We do this through a concept called emotional attunement. It's the art of bringing two people into harmony by being aware of and responsive to each other's emotional needs. We all crave this connection, especially in primary caregiving relationships like with parents or caregivers. When we receive emotional attunement, we feel seen, heard, and understood, which sets the foundation for healing and wholeness.[54]

We commonly speak about physical ailments but prefer to leave our emotions out of the conversation. Yet, one of the most courageous steps is admitting we're struggling.

However, when emotional attunement is absent, and you take that brave step, it can have devastating effects. Without a secure attachment to an emotionally attuned person, we can feel disconnected, invisible, and out of sync with the world around us, causing further trauma, which results in various coping mechanisms such as emotional distance, obsessive control, or codependency, just to name a few.

The good news is that emotional attunement can be developed and learned. It starts with being present, actively listening, and acknowledging each other's emotions. It requires vulnerability and a willingness to connect on a deeper level. With practice and intention, we can all become more emotionally attuned and build more profound, fulfilling relationships with those we love.

I don't think any of us expect the loneliness within suffering. We often fight our battles alone. It is not because friends and family don't try to help. Unfortunately, despite their best efforts, humans struggle to provide the emotional attunement we desperately need in each other. It's painful not to be heard and understood.

Rather than reaching out for support, we often shield ourselves by building distance, detaching, exerting control, or fostering codependency. Unfortunately, this only amplifies brokenness and hinders the healing process. We often turn to external sources for healing, peace, and joy. Whether it's binge-watching Netflix, engaging in excessive use of social

---

54 van der Kolk, *The Body Keeps the Score*.

media, consuming alcohol, or overworking, we seek anything to fill the void and escape from the pain.

Our need to be codependent and detach ourselves is nothing new. In Jeremiah 2:13, God brought this accusation against his people: *"My people have committed two evils: they have forsaken me, the fountain of living waters, and hewed out cisterns for themselves, broken cisterns that can hold no water."*

In a land where scarcity and uncertainty loom, the concept of living water becomes even more profound. A gushing spring provides a constant source of calm, precise nourishment. In the context of ancient Israel, these springs were not mere luxuries but *lifelines*. A river symbolizes reliability, one that will quench thirst and restore weary souls, unlike cisterns, which were man-made based on gathering rainfall to survive the dry season.

Cisterns have their faults. They are prone to contamination, their waters tainted with impurities. And oh, how they teetered on the edge of scarcity! If rain didn't come, reservoirs would dwindle, leaving those who depended on them uncertain, longing, and in danger.

A cracked cistern, a vessel unable to hold water, reminds us that the cisterns we dig don't contain enough water to sustain us effectively. The very things we attempt to use to fill the void will only leave us longing for more. It's the difference between drinking a glass of water from a rain barrel and drinking directly from a mountain stream. The rain barrel may be enough for the moment, but the mountain stream provides an unlimited supply of freshwater and can even be used to fill the rain barrel.

Reflecting on the symbolism of living water versus cisterns calls us to examine our lives. How often do we seek fulfillment and sustenance in things that will never fill our souls? How frequently have we relied on temporary fixes and earthly wells that eventually run dry to avoid vulnerability? Are we building our cisterns to avoid the pain?

Over the years, I have dug a cistern of self-reliance, believing I could navigate through grief and trauma solely by my strength and wisdom. I thought that if only I could do more for myself and my family, all the trauma would go away. Rather than turning toward God, I forged ahead, determined to control every aspect of life, fearing vulnerability and dependency within relationships. I dragged myself out of bed each day, looking for peace and joy through Netflix, social media, and other people, only to discover that this self-made well quickly ran dry, leaving me weary and drained. It's like putting a band-aid on a gaping wound, temporarily stopping the bleeding but not addressing the underlying problem (and, as we've discussed, prone to infection).

Most of us dig the cistern of avoidance through "Christianized numbing," believing it's a sign of weakness and lack of faith to admit our pain. We push the pain away, thinking it will eventually fade if we serve others and praise God enough. "After all, my pain isn't as bad as others," we tell ourselves. We shift our focus on serving enough and being thankful our circumstances aren't as dire as others, believing this will heal the wounds. But instead, we build walls around our hearts, shielding them from the rawness of grief, afraid that entirely embracing the suffering will consume us.

Often, the more we try to suppress the grief, the more it seeps into every aspect of our lives, manifesting as emotional numbness and resentment. If we don't scream, our bodies will. The cracks in our self-made cisterns cause grief to slowly infiltrate our lives, affecting our relationships, our bodies and sense of self, and our ability to find meaning in the pain and suffering.

Knowing our flawed attempts, God invites us to experience His living water. It requires surrendering our reliance on the broken cisterns we've depended on and turning toward the everlasting springs of grace and abundance we find in a relationship with God. We can slowly open ourselves to the transformative power of the living water, allowing it to heal our wounds, cleanse our souls, and quench our deepest longings.

In Genesis 21, we find Hagar, a woman lost in the vast wilderness of despair for the second time. Fourteen years earlier, she wandered with a heavy heart and weary feet; however, this time, she'd been cast back into the wilderness with her son. She felt abandoned by God and was looking for peace, a glimmer of hope amidst her suffering. Instead of turning towards God, she turned towards a cistern of despair, causing her to focus on her lack. She'd lost all hope and began to feel sorry for herself. Oh, the anguish she must have felt; her despair clouded her vision of the works of God.

Then, as the drinking water ran dry and the sun started to dip under the horizon, in her despair, she sat her son under a bush. Sitting opposite him, she said, *"Let me not look on the death of the child"* (Genesis 21:16).

Little did she know that even in her darkest moments, God was working behind the scenes, orchestrating a divine plan. Oh, the anguish she must have felt, the desperation that clouded her vision, keeping her from realizing that relief was near. Instead of focusing on where God was, Hagar focused on where God wasn't.

Was I doing the same? Was I so focused on where I thought God wasn't working that I was missing where His presence gave me life?

*"...and then [Hagar] lifted up her voice and wept"* (Genesis 21:17).

Hagar embraced her pain and sorrow, weeping as a testament to her love for her son. Her grief was not a sign of weakness but rather a reflection of the deep connections she forged and the immense capacity of her heart to love.

Through her tears, Hagar found the courage to confront her grief head-on. She allowed herself to feel the waves of emotion as they washed over her. In those moments of vulnerability, little did Hagar know that an encounter awaited her that would change everything.

In Genesis 21:17, God sweetly asks, *"What troubles you, Hagar?"* God's question allowed Hagar to feel the reality of her situation while also revealing His compassion for her pain. God is not interrogating us when He asks a question; He's drawing us closer.

Once again, God sees and hears. The angel of the Lord finds Hagar and comforts her: *"Do not be afraid; God has heard the boy crying...Lift the boy up and take him by the hand, for I will make him a great nation"* (Genesis 211:17-18). Then, God revealed His promise and provision, unveiling a wellspring of hope hidden from Hagar's weary eyes.

*"Then God opened her eyes, and she saw a well of water"* (vs 19).

I wonder how often we fail to see a well because we focus on the despair of our situation.

You are, at your very essence, not defined by your circumstances. In

161

her despair, Hagar failed to see the life-giving source she needed to forge ahead. Hagar embraced the reality of her circumstances, but God opened her eyes to His love.

In her moments of brokenness, Hagar realized her grief was not a barrier separating her from God's love but a gateway to a deeper connection. She discovered a reservoir of strength she never knew she possessed in the depths of her sorrow. Through God, she tapped into a wellspring of resilience that could carry her through, even though the weight of loss threatened to overwhelm her.

It's not our vulnerability of crying over the reality of our circumstances that keeps us from feeling God's love; it's that we embrace despair.

As we follow Hagar's example, we'll discover a resilience that surpasses our wildest imaginings—a strength born from the unwavering belief that she was never alone. The only way to keep experiencing the wellspring of life is to focus on God's never-ending love for us.

In Hagar's story, we see echoes of our journeys through grief. Like Hagar, we also wander in a wilderness of sorrow, often feeling lost, abandoned, and unseen. The weight of grief is insurmountable, causing us to question the promises of God. Like Hagar, focusing on our despair obscures our vision of God's works. All we feel is the weight of uncertainty. Yet, in the depths of her sorrow, God saw her pain, struggles, and longings, and today, He sees all of ours, too. With tender compassion, God revealed a well, a hidden oasis amidst the barrenness of Hagar's circumstances. Suddenly, her eyes opened, and she beheld the very source of life she had yearned for:

*"Living Water."*

Oh, how breathtaking it must have been, the dawning realization that her hope was within reach. In that instant, her vulnerability transformed into strength, her weariness into resilience. Hagar drank deeply from the well of grace, quenching her thirst for water and experiencing the renewal of her spirit.

Hagar discovered that even in the wilderness of her life, God had not abandoned her. Instead, He saw her pain and chose to meet her there, revealing His presence in the most unexpected ways. Through her journey of affliction, she learned to trust in divine timing, surrender her desperate grasp for control, and lean on God's unwavering faithfulness.

The story of Hagar reminds us that even when we are blind to the wellsprings of healing around us, God sees us and beckons us toward the source of our restoration. He longs to unveil the hidden wells in our lives, those wells of comfort, healing, and purpose that may go unnoticed until His divine revelation opens our eyes.

Buried in frustration and despair, I collapsed, exhausted from trying to figure it out. Exhausted from worrying and wondering if Douglas will always have an addiction, I asked God to show me these hidden wells in my own life.

Just as Hagar discovered a well in the desert, I also encountered "well" moments along my path. These wells lay hidden within the barrenness of my grief, emerging when I least expected them. They were the small, tender mercies that whispered of God's presence, reminding me I wasn't alone. They were in the Wednesday night talks with my close friends. They were in the meals shared with my husband and shared laughter with my teenagers.

In everyday life, we find these wells of God's never-ending love. Suppose you're willing to see them within healthy relationships—a friend's note that strengthens your soul or an unexpected gift. Whether it's a sunset, a child's laugh, or a gentle hug from a friend—they're all filled with unexpected beauty and love. Beauty and love broke through the darkness, and I savored these "well" moments, bringing a temporary respite.

May we be like Hagar in our moments of despair and doubt. Let us remain open to the possibility of hidden wells, trusting that God's timing is perfect and His provision abundant. And when the veil lifts, may we drink deeply from the wells of grace, finding strength, hope, and a renewed sense of purpose to continue our path with resilience and unwavering faith.

In the depths of our suffering, it can feel as if God is distant, hidden from our weary eyes. We question His presence, wondering why He allows such pain to pierce our souls. The weight of our burdens presses upon us, and we strain to perceive any sign of His hand at work.

God's presence becomes even more profound in these moments. Even when tears obscure our sight and our hearts ache with unanswered questions, there's an invitation to a deeper understanding of faith.

In the crucible of hardship, our spirits are refined like precious metal, allowing us to learn to endure, persevere, and find strength within ourselves that we never knew existed. I've even experienced creativity blossoming, searching for new ways to navigate pain. In these dark corners of my life, my writing emerged.

My journaling became the avenue for introspection, and I began to unravel the wounds of my heart. I'd find myself anticipating the moments of slipping away and pouring out my heart on those pages of my journal. Journaling is my creative way of hashing out my purpose, values, and deepest desires. The vulnerability within those pages is the gateway to discovering the depths of my emotions and the dormant questions. Creative outlets can illuminate those "hidden wells," sparking hope.

In this sacred space of self-reflection, I encountered the hand of God, tenderly guiding me toward Living Water. In the chambers of my heart, transformation unfolded, revealing how the trauma had caused a self-destructive inner narrative.

Being honest about this narrative sowed seeds of change.

Finding creative avenues for our suffering allows for divine transformation, releasing the shackles of complacency and surrendering to the discomfort of self-discovery. We can peel back the layers of conditioning, unearthing beliefs and patterns that have shaped us. We can allow God's grace to reshape our perspectives and attitudes in this vulnerable exploration. For instance, we may recognize the need to forgive ourselves for past wrongs and let go of negative self-talk, freeing us from perpetual self-criticism and guilt.

As we navigate this introspective path, we realize that change is not a sudden revelation but a gradual change. It's more like a patient dance of self-discovery, where insights emerge like delicate brushstrokes on a canvas. Then, in the gentle whispers of our hearts, we will hear God's voice, guiding us toward our most authentic selves and opening us up to hope once again.

Hope, even though elusive at times, remains our steadfast companion. It whispers, reminding us a greater story is unfolding. It tells us our pain is not in vain, there is purpose in our journey, and our wounds will one day transform into sources of healing for ourselves and others.

On the other side of suffering, hope reminds us that our story is still being written, and a purpose we cannot yet comprehend awaits us.

While we may not always see the immediate workings of God in our suffering, we can trust He is present, walking alongside us in the shadows. His love surrounds us, even when it feels most distant. He weeps with us, holds us in our despair, and carries us when we cannot take another step.

Let us embrace the vulnerability of our suffering, knowing that through our brokenness, we find strength. Let us cultivate a resilient spirit, aware our struggles shape us into compassionate and empathetic beings. Hagar's story teaches us that even in the wilderness of our lives, there is hope. It reminds us that our vulnerability is not a weakness but a gateway to transformation and growth.

As we embrace our journey with vulnerability, introspection, and resilience, we find peace in knowing even when we cannot see the way forward God is working behind the scenes, guiding us toward a future filled with purpose and promise.

Like Hagar, may we have the courage to abandon our cistern of despair and embrace the vulnerability ourselves to feel deeply. May we find strength in our brokenness and resilience in our pain. May we trust that God's presence is steadfast in our grief, offering comfort, healing, and hope.

Today may be heavy, but tomorrow holds the promise of renewal. In the dance between exhaustion and hope, we will discover the strength to rise again, embrace life's uncertainties, and find solace in knowing our weariness is not in vain.

There is hope. I've learned by recognizing our vulnerabilities and how the journey has wounded us, we can become more empathetic and attuned to the needs of others. We can learn to offer safety, connection, and healing to those around us. It's a difficult journey, but one that is worth taking. We may never fully overcome our wounds, but by showing up for each other and offering love and support, we can satisfy our thirst. We invite God's transformative touch by turning our gaze inward and examining the depths of our hearts. Then, we are better equipped to recognize our strengths and weaknesses, enabling us to live more fully in the present with a more profound sense of purpose.

Each day, we are one step closer to becoming the best version of ourselves, rooted in authenticity and connected to God.

As we drink from the well of divine love and grace, we discover a source that never runs dry—a sustenance we crave, the refreshment that renews our spirits. Taking refuge in living water offers a pathway to resilience, for it is only through surrendering to the divine flow that we can find strength beyond our comprehension.

Through these vulnerable moments, I realize my strength and resilience for the first time. As I embrace and surrender my brokenness, I discover its transformative power, which carries me through the exhaustion. Unexpectedly, suffering has become the raw material from which I find strength and wisdom. It's the very thing that has allowed me to connect to others with empathy.

The lack of relief and answers can be disheartening, but there's an invitation to embrace the unknown within this void. Without certainty, there's a calling to surrender and trust God. Though it may be challenging, there is a profound beauty in relinquishing control and finding peace in the mystery.

In tender vulnerability, I acknowledge my weariness while remaining open to the lessons suffering brings. I surrender to the unknown, trusting that a more remarkable story is being written. I lean into the fatigue, knowing that it is through these weary moments that resilience is born.

## DIGGING DEEPER:

1. How does embracing the wellspring of God's divine love and grace sustain and refresh our spirits during trial?

2. How do you navigate the disheartening moments of suffering when relief and answers seem elusive? What does embracing the unknown and trusting God mean in those times?

# CHAPTER 13

## LIMPING WITH GRIEF AND DANCING WITH JOY

*"The walls we build around us to keep sadness out also keep out joy."*[55]

My friend Angel penned these words after losing her brother to suicide at only fifty-two years of age:

"I usually don't tell anyone how bad I feel—confused, tormented, lonely. My eyes hurt, along with my head. I want to reach out and scream from the rooftops, but I can't. My life, which I hold, waits for me, yet I don't trust myself. I'm too needy, too demanding, too sad. I think I want silence, a quiet place. I wonder if the silence would make the torture seem less torturous. My heart aches because I feel guilty, craving the moments to be still or have silence. The life I have is anything but quiet.

I miss my brother. His presence, being, breathing, part of our circle, the bloodline of our existence. The age gap of nine years older than me made him feel distant at times, but I knew he was always there.

Now, he is not.

---

[55] Kay Warren, *Choose Joy: Because Happiness Isn't Enough* (Ada, MI: Baker Publishing Group, 2012), 142.

People tend to faint when they become physically and emotionally overwhelmed. I saw a lady faint at the funeral of her husband once. Even though my thoughts and feelings are so great they swallow me up at times, I don't feel like fainting; I want to run. I want to run as fast and hard as possible until I am no more. I imagine myself melting into the hot black asphalt, a pool of liquid that fills the cracks and then disintegrates into nothing.

Still being here without him, holding the loss, my face hurts. It holds the grudges, weak eyes, and endless tears back so I can be what I need to be in my life. I must pick up kids, feed them, and care for them while working at a computer, wishing, hoping, and praying my body, heart, and mind will be still for a moment. I need to catch my breath. I need to process my brother's death. This loss, the pain of him not being here anymore. And with him, he took what once was. I want to cry, but I don't have time. I feel the water pooling in my eyes as the oven bell dings, reminding me to remove the chicken from the oven. I hear my daughter mumble sweet things to her baby doll playing in the other room. The boys play outside, anticipating the great things for the day. I tell myself to wrap it up. It is only a fleeting moment.

I stick it back in the depths of my stomach, pushing it deep inside. I imagine duct-taping the mouth of my grief for another day, another time. I tell the sadness to disappear from my mind, almost like sticking a child in the corner for a timeout. I know my grief will not be silent forever, but I must go for now. There are things to do, kids to take somewhere fun like the pool, and clothes to wash and dry. A pain shoots across my head from one side to the other, but I ignore it. I will pretend it is all okay. I'm fine.

My breath hurts, but I'm still breathing. My eyes are sore, but I can see. The soreness in my body tends to linger way too long, but I can rise again. I miss my brother, yet I am unsure what I miss. But I miss him still the same. I wonder if he knew how much I loved him, if he knew what he meant to our lives."

A few months ago, Angel was going about her day as usual, tending to her children and the endless duties of the house and work, unaware that she'd receive a phone call from her mother with the devastating news that rearranged her entire world. That fast, horrific reality set into an ordinary day. His disease got the best of him, and he thought he had no choice.

Unfortunately, our friendship has weathered several storms like this. Most Wednesday nights, while the kids are at church, we sit with another friend at a local restaurant to catch up. Our conversations are real and raw. Sometimes, we laugh till our sides hurt, and sometimes, we cry until no tears are left. It's okay not to be okay or feel strong or put together. We've made a pack to avoid phrases like "I'm okay" or "I'm fine." If we're struggling, we don't hide it. If one of us feels depressed or sad, we describe it. If we feel anxious or worried about something, we voice it. Nothing is off the table.

Not only does suffering make up our friendship, but also mining for joy. We've unexpectedly found joy in our suffering, strengthening our friendship even more. It's true. If our friendship were a club, we would call it the *Beaten But Not Struck Down* club. Want to join?!

We've journeyed through some pretty hefty stuff between the three of us. Anything from suicide to addiction and cancer—it seems we're constantly wrangling cancer. These life-altering events are not two-hour heart-wrenching movies from which we can exit and enjoy a fairytale happy ending. The complexity of our realities does not come wrapped up in a pretty red bow. Sadly, our fairytale ending does not exist.

While everyone else is mapping out the future, saving the world, we're hugging each other, barely holding on most days. But as we navigate suffering and grief, we've gotten good at joy-mining.

Our Wednesday night talks taught us we can't rank or minimize each other's suffering. We, instead, embrace it with love. Despite our shared losses, we have realized that grief transforms our dance into a limping stumble as we mingle with the shadows of grief. So, we've embraced that grieving is necessary for healing and experiencing joy.

Moving too quickly through grief without allowing ourselves to feel the depth of sadness only limits us from feeling the depth of joy. The reality is we can't experience the depth of joy if we haven't felt the depth of sorrow.

During our collective grief, we've discovered we each grieve differently. The complexities of loss, especially when faced with the aftermath of suicide, bring forth a tangled web of emotions. Angel realized she couldn't grieve her brother's death like she grieved her father-in-law. Whenever death is accompanied by trauma, such as suicide, a whole range of emotions is evoked. It demands attention, urging us to confront the depth of emotions.

With a vulnerable heart, she's allowed herself to unravel on our Wednesday nights. Shedding tears and allowing God and friends to witness her pain wash away the raw ache of grief. She discovered freedom when she refused to let her feelings own her.

Friends, I cannot begin to tell you how important it is to name what matters to you, how you're feeling, and what's weighing you down. Sharing our stories, questions, and regrets in the safety of friendship brings peace and freedom. There's no need to appear strong; we discover strength in our vulnerability.

Finding a safe place for grief is essential to finding healing and joy. What sends us into the deepest part of the wilderness is processing grief alone and refusing to stay in a relationship with God and others. When we try to control all the hurt feelings and take care of ourselves, we exile ourselves to the wilderness.

Those Wednesday nights peeled back the curtain on our journey, helping us to see the path is not linear from darkness to light but a dance between limping with grief and dancing with joy. We can acknowledge the sorrow while holding onto the glimmers of hope. We can embrace the truth that joy doesn't erase our grief, and grief doesn't extinguish the flame of joy. We can be free knowing it's a delicate balance.

It can be a vulnerable place to accept that grief and joy coexist; however, allowing ourselves to experience both is liberating. Joy ushers in the hope that good things can still happen and the future looks less glum.

The wounds of grief may never fully heal, but they are a testament to our capacity for love and joy.

I stand there in disbelief the day I wake up after Douglas's eighteenth birthday and realize he's gone again. He chose to chase a high over the warmth of family. My mind is still unable to comprehend his addiction. Standing there washing dishes, crying, reeling with anger, and feeling the sharp edge of grief, my four-year-old daughter brings me what she thinks is a flower in a styrofoam cup, except we adults know it as a weed.

At this moment, I face a choice. I can either cling to bitterness and resentment or dismantle the barriers and welcome joy into my life. Can I muster a smile as I embrace my daughter with enthusiasm? Can I believe that something beautiful will sprout from this small dixie cup? Or will I persist in holding onto bitterness and convince myself that nothing will grow?

Joy feels delicate and exposed—vulnerable. Is it permissible for me to allow myself to experience joy?

Today, I opt to carry my grief with grace, allowing it to shape me without dictating our existence. In our brokenness, I've realized that our hearts can hold both sorrow and joy, to sway between grief and gratitude. Gradually, I allow a smile to form on my lips, trusting that something will indeed begin to bloom in that tiny cup.

It's easy to think you'll always be sad and the tears will never stop, but over time, grief becomes a part of you. It doesn't go away. It mingles with joy and gratitude.

Joy doesn't come easy when you're fighting through grief and trauma. In James 1:2 (NLT) is a startling command: *"When troubles come your way, consider it an opportunity for great joy"*. Experiencing great joy is not my first thought when trouble comes. My knee-jerk reaction is to moan and complain about everything that has gone wrong. But I know now that I've had it all wrong. If life caves in, a loved one passes, the rug gets pulled out from under you, and all you have is God, that's enough because that's where the joy is found—in Him.

Bottom line: Joy is a choice. It's not dependent on circumstances.

In his book *How Can It Be All Right*, Lewis Smedes writes, "You and I were created for joy, and if we miss it, we miss the reason for our existence! Moreover, the reason Jesus Christ lived and died on earth was to restore us to the joy we have lost...His Spirit comes to us with the power to believe that joy is our birthright because the Lord has made this day for us."[56]

We quickly forget joy is our inheritance as children of God. It's not for a select few whose lives are going well.

For those of us who have experienced trauma and significant loss know joy is not the same thing as happiness. It's not a series of good days versus a series of bad days. Our lack of joy does not result from a lack of human effort. If true, our faith would stand on works instead of grace. And that verse in Nehemiah urging that "the joy of the Lord is our strength" can be pretty oppressive when you're not feeling too happy.

"Joy is the settled assurance that God is in control of all the details of my life, the quiet confidence that ultimately everything is going to be all right, and the determined choice to praise God in all things."[57] I wrote this definition on a notecard and taped it up in the kitchen, where I can see it daily. This reminder becomes my lifeline for everyday life.

Joy is not a happy passing moment. *Joy is an assured presence of Jesus.*

I once believed life's journey resembled a landscape of hills and valleys—a constant cycle of highs and lows. But over the last few years, I've discovered a profound truth: Life is not a mere see-sawing between peaks and troughs; instead, it unfolds like parallel train tracks, where joy and sorrow are inseparable. Every day dawns with the promise of something beautiful– a glimmer of hope ignites the track of joy.

Yet grief's track stretches before me, a path weaving through my existence, reminding me of the fragility of life. However, this track runs alongside joy as I confront heartache, shattered dreams, and the weight of sorrow threatening to overwhelm me. Joy and grief are inextricably linked!

In pursuit of happiness, I often attempt to outsmart the track of sorrow. I'd pour my energy into the path of joy as if I could make the

---

[56] Lewis Smedes, *How Can It Be All Right When Everything Is All Wrong?* Rev. ed. (Wheaton: Harold Shaw, 1999), 27, 43.
[57] Warren, *Choose Joy*, 31.

sorrow track vanish by sheer willpower, positive thinking, or denial. Joy and sorrow run together throughout the fabric of our daily lives.

As we embrace joy and sorrow, we can discover an inexplicable awareness of beauty, creating joy in the depths of pain. Even as tears flow and our hearts ache, we are not blind to the exquisite moments surrounding us, like a sunset. While suffering, we can find ourselves extra attuned to these delicate beauties of life—the kindness of a stranger, the warmth of a loved one's embrace, or the gentle whisper of nature. In the middle of a grief-stricken period, the beauty of a single flower can evoke a sense of joy despite our sorrow. Like tender flower petals strewn along the track, these moments bring color and vibrancy to our lives.

To deny sorrow is to deny joy, for it is within the depths of grief that true joy takes place. In these depths, we learn to navigate the complexities of our emotions and hold space for joy and sorrow. Through the dance of pain and beauty, we discover the true essence of our humanity.

So, I write today with a vulnerable heart, acknowledging life's tracks of joy and grief run side by side. I embrace the sorrows, for they illuminate the joys that make life worth living. Amidst the pain, it's important we cherish the beautiful everyday moments because that's where we find joy.

As I journey forward, I hold the paradox close—joy and sorrow forever meshed together. And through it all, I remain steadfast in the belief that every step taken, every tear shed, and every smile shared is a testament to the richness of life itself.

The bond of joy and sorrow is our strength. As vulnerable as it is, we can't shy away from grief or joy, for they complement each other and are an essential part of the human experience. It's similar to how the light of day can only be fully appreciated when we have experienced the dark of night and how the song of a bird can sound sweeter after the silence of the night. The contrast of joy and sorrow makes life richer and more profound.

In efforts to offer comfort, an old cliche is said, "God will never give you more than you can handle." I have a few thoughts on this statement, but I'll start with this: it's a lot of nonsense! This remark claims that God wants us to confront harsh and unbearable conditions, and we should buck up to deal with whatever comes our way. I once heard a pastor say, "It's like a child running out into oncoming traffic and expecting them to just deal with it on their own." It's a hazardous and harmful concept since it can lead to intense feelings of guilt and inadequacy when we cannot cope with life's difficulties. It may sound lovely to our ears, but it can lead to deception in our hearts.

We want these words to bring comfort, but they have no truth. More times than I can count, I have experienced more than I can handle. Despite my best efforts, I have nothing left to give because God *does* give us more than we can handle! And it's in this lack that we experience more of Him.

Because we avoid discussing grief, we often have a distorted perception of what it should look like in our daily lives. Grief defies containment; it's unpredictable, insidious, and imposing. It's an unexplainable force that demands attention when least expected. Grief doesn't conform to a box, and it manifests not only in response to physical death but also in the face of various losses, such as relocating to a different state and mourning everything left behind.

The journey through grief isn't standardized; sometimes, it takes years to navigate. What I've come to understand is that everyone experiences grief uniquely. We each need to embrace the roller coaster of grief, acknowledging that, even if we're uncertain about what's considered normal or right, it's a journey we all must undertake for healing and forward movement.

I don't expect grief to show up today. My father passed away several years ago, and the weight of his death felt almost unbearable on my birthday this year. I had experienced bouts of despair, but this morning, I found myself submerged.

As I roll over in bed, the realization hits me, "I won't hear my dad wish me a happy birthday today." I attempt to push the thought away with gratitude, reminding myself of my blessings—a kid-free trip from my husband and the promise of more unexpected joys. Shouldn't that be enough? My attempt at gratitude works for a while because, really, who wants to be sad on their birthday? Except, gratitude is not a magic wand we wave to make life easier.

I get out of bed, grab my coffee, and try to convince myself that I should be happy. The kids shower me with gifts, and my husband discusses our dinner date.

I don't quite grasp the relationship between joy and grief until my mom walks in my back door at lunchtime with a bouquet of flowers and a gift. It's a pleasant surprise to enjoy lunch together on my actual birthday. It is a pleasant surprise—I can't recall the last time that happened. Due to her prolonged struggle to get pregnant, she always told me I was a miracle baby. We laugh about how my dad ran out and bought everything pink after my birth. She talks about finding her new normal. We both tear up, remembering my father.

As we talk, I feel the presence of grief and joy together, mingling, not replacing each other. It's a delicate dance. Nobody tells you that throwing up a shield to keep out grief will also keep out joy. Joy doesn't replace grief.

Joy mingles with grief.

What do I wish I had known sooner?

Being grateful doesn't fix grief. Just as joy doesn't replace grief, gratitude doesn't either. They abide together. Gratitude softens the grieving process. It's not about looking on the bright side to numb the pain. It's about being thankful for our small moments of joy and connection, even in grief. Gratitude grounds us to the present moment, allowing us to see the beauty of life so our emotions can't overwhelm us. Gratitude gives us the courage to move forward in difficult times, knowing we can find joy despite hardship.

God created us as complex beings capable of experiencing both sadness and joy. Grieving with hope involves consistently bringing your feelings to the feet of Jesus, immersing yourself in the Word, reminding yourself of the truth, and staying connected to a community of believers.

Even when it's challenging, intentionally seek joy and peace amid sorrow. Both can coexist within you, aiding in the healthy processing of pain.

Remember, *"Weeping may endure for a night, but joy cometh in the morning."* [58]

**Harmony Amidst the Heartache: The Transformative Power of Worship**

When tragedy strikes, one or two things happen: people either turn toward God or away from God. The pain and suffering either bring them to their knees or jerks them up, carrying them away from God.

We have a choice: we can stand back in pride, questioning God, demanding answers and a quick fix out of this suffering, or we can choose to trust in God's character. Whether we acknowledge Him or not, I am confident God is with us.

The capacity to limp with grief and dance with joy raises up the faith to sustain us in the pain of uncertainty and lead us toward hope.

In those sacred moments of surrender, when my heart is open and vulnerable before God, I've realized that worship is the bridge that spans the chasm between grief and joy. Worship is the melody that weaves us through the tapestry of life, carrying the harmonies of sorrow and joy in perfect unison.

In the weeks and months after the fire, I find that worship enables me to feel His tangible presence, reminding me of His peace and joy that never leaves us.

Our family motto became, "We may be sad, but we're not going to stay stuck." We keep moving forward in faith.

A few days after the dreadful day of the house fire, I wrote in my journal, "Our family will prosper. We are not victims of a fire." Several weeks later, my husband and I hosted a worship night on the slab of our

---

[58] Psalm 30:5, KJV

once-built house to declare this truth. We called our pastor to organize all the details, and to our surprise, so many others were willing to declare His promises with us. Witnessing how many people showed up to encourage us and proclaim His goodness served as a reminder we're never victims of our circumstances.

As the sun sets, our family, church community, and close friends gather on the slab where our house once sat. We're not in a grand cathedral or a majestic sanctuary, but God's presence is there just the same.

Worship music fills the air, resonating deep within our souls and awakening a sense of unity. Our hearts declare His goodness.

We can stand firm in the truth of His promises.

Lifting our voices in worship announces to the enemy there will be a reckoning day. A day when God will carry through with His promise: *"He will wipe every tear from their eyes. There will be no more death or mourning or crying or pain."* (Revelation 21:4)

Even when the enemy comes in and seems to take everything, Have no fear. Our God redeems: *"And the LORD restored the fortunes of Job, when he had prayed for his friends. And the LORD gave Job twice as much as he had before."* (Job 42:10).

Our God is faithful!

In the depths of grief, I find peace and joy as I pour out my heart before the One who holds every tear, every ache, and every shattered dream. I discover a safe space in the worship to lament, grieve, and be raw and vulnerable. I am here, met with compassion. Grief is not a sign of weakness but a testament to the depth of love shared and lost.

Sometimes, you must sing the Truth to remind yourself the promise is coming.

That night in the open air, we declare our unwavering trust in a God who never fails, who turns our mourning into dancing and strengthens us in our weakness. Even during the darkest night, a glimmer of light emerges. The gentle whisper of hope reminds us of the beauty within Christ. Joy doesn't extinguish grief but instead finds its strength in the midst of it through worship. It is a resilient flame that refuses to be snuffed out by life's trials.

Worship invites us to dance joyfully even when our hearts are heavy with sorrow. It beckons us to celebrate the goodness of life, find gratitude in the smallest moments, and embrace the beauty surrounding us.

In the embrace of worship, I discover the resilience to rise above the weight of despair and to find strength in the face of adversity. In this intimate space, hope began to bud, breaking through the cracks of my brokenness. Through worship, I find the resilience to embrace the journey ahead, knowing I don't walk it alone.

The flickering beams of the last sunlight illuminate our faces, revealing tears of joy and determination. We hold hands, united in purpose and ready to face whatever challenges lay ahead, knowing when we stand in His presence, the enemy has no access to God's steadfast love! It's forever and constantly chasing after us. Our declaration serves as a lighthouse, guiding us through the storms and reminding us of the unwavering love that binds us together.

As the worship night ends, a sense of peace settles upon us. We know this declaration is a fleeting moment and a commitment that will shape our lives. In the days to come, we will stumble and falter, but we will always return to this sacred space, to the remainder of our declaration, and to the assurance that God's grace is sufficient. It's down in the valley that we find intimacy with God.

Aaron's sister Miriam knew this intimacy with God by choosing to worship through her fear and anxiety. As we read in Exodus 15:20, Miriam worshiped with the other women after crossing the Red Sea on dry land with a tambourine.

Forced to vacate her home in darkness, Miriam probably needed more time to pack. Pharaoh could change his mind any minute about letting God's people go (which he had done several times already). Knowing they had to get out quickly, Miriam moved frantically.

Can you imagine? "Let's see... I'll pack clothes, barley, the unrisen bread, oils, maybe some honey, and oh yeah....and my tambourine."

A tambourine? It's just the thing I pack in my suitcase, too.

I don't know if all the women had tambourines, but Miriam did because she believed in the power of worship. It's what keeps us limping with grief and dancing with joy.

Worship keeps our hearts surrendered to whatever comes our way. It keeps our eyes focused on the One who holds the whole earth in His hands. Worship opens our spirits up to what God is doing, and in return, we lay down our plans and desires.

Friend, do you have your tambourine ready to worship when the nights come, and your heart is weary from not seeing growth?

In moments of worship, I find the strength to surrender to the unknown. In moments of worship, we see a glimpse of Heaven on earth, allowing us to continue. This worship night became a catalyst for transformation in me and my family.

We honor our grief journey by embracing the dance of grief and joy. In this delicate balance, we can discover the fullness of life's beauty.

---

## DIGGING DEEPER:

1. Listen to your favorite worship song and allow your praise to be a weapon. Sometimes, you must sing your beliefs to remind yourself the promise is coming.

2. Write the definition of joy and tape it somewhere you can see it often, reminding yourself joy is not equivalent to happiness.

3. Keep a gratitude journal and document all the moments of beauty you see during the day. Allow these moments to be reminders that joy and grief can coexist.

# CHAPTER 14

## EMBRACING THE PHYSICAL SIDE OF GRIEF AND TRAUMA

*"Neuroscience research shows that the only way we can change how we feel is by becoming aware of our inner experience and learning to befriend what is going inside ourselves."*[59]

One day, as I stand in the coffee section of the grocery store, my mind and body are heavy with grief. The array of coffee creamers stares back at me, each representing an impossible choice. Decision fatigue has taken hold of me, amplifying the anxiety coursing through my veins. The toll of grief on my body is undeniable—a combination of exhaustion, decision fatigue, memory loss, and, don't forget, those darn bladder spasms.

It seems absurd to be so overwhelmed by something as simple as choosing a creamer, but grief has a way of infiltrating every aspect of our lives. It can cast a dark cloud over our ability to make even the most mundane decisions.

As I stand there, my eyes blur over the options before me. I can't help but feel the weight of each choice magnified. It isn't just about coffee

---

[59] van der Kolk, *The Body Keeps the Score*, 206.

anymore; it reflects my daily internal struggle. Every decision feels like a monumental task, a potential misstep that could further unravel my fragile state.

The anxiety accompanying grief is relentless. It tightens its grip around my chest, making it difficult to breathe and even harder to make decisions. My mind races with thoughts of what-ifs and second-guessing, leaving me paralyzed in a sea of indecision.

At that moment, I realize the toll grief has taken on my body. It goes beyond the emotional pain, seeping into every fiber now affecting my physical and mental well-being. The weight of sorrow drains my energy, clouds my judgment, and leaves me in perpetual darkness.

I've lost my joy. I'm not smiling as much and I feel like a shell—a vessel weathered by grief, exhaustion etched into my being. As I sit there, staring at the coffee creamers, unable to make a simple decision, I see the physical struggle manifesting the storm within me. It reflects the anxiety and turmoil that accompany grief, weighing heavy on my soul and leaving its mark on my body.

Trauma goes beyond the superficial—it reaches deep into the core of our being, reaping havoc on our emotions and bodies.

In the journey to healing from grief, there's the importance of addressing the physical side—the part that often goes unnoticed or is pushed aside during emotional turmoil. It becomes a lesson in self-care and self-compassion, a reminder that tending to the body is vital to our healing process.

Healing means recognizing grief's toll on my body and allowing space and grace to heal. It means seeing the connection between our emotions and physical bodies because honoring our bodies is honoring our grief.

So, take a deep breath, dear traveler, and be fully present in these last two chapters. Embrace the vulnerability, for it is a doorway to transformation. I invite you to join me in unraveling the physical side of grief, knowing that the other side awaits a glimmer of hope and a renewed sense of self.

In tragic moments, our brains protect us during trauma.

Our house fire shattered my sense of safety and left me grappling with the physical aftermath of grief, which consumed every part of me.

A whirlwind of chaos and fear circled my mind as the flames engulfed our home. In the commotion, my brain shut down certain aspects of my cognition to shield it from the overwhelming trauma. It is as if a protective barrier formed, protecting me from the total weight of the horror unfolding before my eyes.

I later heard from my sister-in-law that my body was there, but my brain was elsewhere.

There were peculiar gaps in my memory the days and weeks after the fire. Despite having etched the details in my mind, I can't recall the specific sequence of events. It's as if my brain carefully placed a curtain over those harrowing moments, shielding me from the raw intensity of the experience. Even today, I can't recall specific events after and during the fire. Gaps in my memory also extend into the times of Douglas's active addiction. It's like I'm trying to remember a dream—however hard I try, I can't break through the fog that has settled over those memories.

Grief and trauma affect the brain, invading the memories and casting a murky haze over the past. Moments that once were vividly in the mind now seem distant, like a faded photograph found in the dusty corner of an attic. Trauma survivors often have difficulty recalling specific details, colors, and emotions from past experiences. Grief and trauma drain the world of color, leaving behind black and white.

Now, months after the fire, my memory still cannot keep track of simple tasks. Each day, it feels like I'm living in a fog. The children often remind me of the things I am apt to forget. Even simple decisions became challenging, such as what to cook for dinner or what to wear. All the everyday choices are also clouded by rebuilding a house, navigating a child in and out of rehab, and lacking sleep. The trauma numbs my mind.

I hang in a tangled web of decision fatigue and memory loss. It's as if my brain is a battleground where grief is waging war on my ability to think clearly. Within this disorienting chaos, I unearth the impact that grief is having on my physical body.

Grief's relentless assault has drained and overwhelmed my mind and body. Grief permeates the heart, mind, and body with its relentless grip. Our bodies become vessels carrying the weight of sorrow—the weariness seeps into our bones, and the knots tighten in our stomachs.

At first, I felt frustrated and confused, wondering why my mind and body were failing me. But with time and research, I now see that this is a God-created mechanism of self-preservation, a way for our wounded minds to protect themselves from being overtaken by the trauma. The delicate balance between remembering and healing is a powerful intricacy of our brains.

Aundi Kolber, in her book *Try Softer*, "In moments of terror, our parasympathetic nervous system, often known as the "rest and digest" mode, reveals another dimension of its intricate workings. While it typically promotes relaxation, it also can plunge our bodies into a frozen state—a coping mechanism when we perceive ourselves trapped with no means of escape. This innate response shields us from real or perceived threats without seeking the approval of our logical minds. The freeze response, appearing on a spectrum, can range from a gentle fog clouding our presence to the extremity of fainting or physical collapse."[60]

When our brain is in this frozen state, we witness the power of our bodies' self-preservation instincts. I love that complex dance between rest and the frozen state -that relies not entirely on fight or flight. It whispers to us the wisdom of adapting, of finding sanctuary in stillness when escape seems impossible.

Recognizing that the frozen state of our brain is not a sign of weakness or failure is crucial. It's a testament to the intricate dance between our bodies and minds, a delicate balance God designed for us when we face overwhelming circumstances. Our instinctual biology, devoid of rational

---

[60] Aundi Kolber, *Try Softer: A Fresh Approach to Move Us out of Anxiety, Stress, and Survival Mode-and into a Life of Connection and Joy* (Downers Grove, IL: InterVarsity Press, 2020).

thought, shields us from the storm, even if it means momentarily disconnecting from our surroundings. Pretty impressive, right?

The mild fog of not feeling present is a protective cocoon when the world becomes too much to bear. It allows us to catch our breath and gather the fragments of our shattered resilience. Yet, on the other end of the spectrum lies the profound vulnerability of physical collapse, a stark reminder of the depths our bodies will go to shield us from the unyielding grip of terror.

To avoid staying stuck, we confront our humanity's fragility, limitations, and intricate details through these frozen states. It is a humbling reminder that God did not create us as infallible creatures. When we unravel the complexities of our parasympathetic response, we can approach ourselves with compassion and understanding.

Let us honor the survival strategy as a testament to God's way of protecting and preserving us. And in that recognition, may we extend the same grace to ourselves as we do to others, knowing that the invisible battles we fight may manifest in ways that challenge our understanding.

Fog-filled minds and bodies warped with grief hold seeds of resilience, which are patiently waiting to sprout. As we navigate our journey, may we cultivate a deep reverence for the intricate wisdom of our bodies, knowing that even in stillness, healing is possible, and transformation emerges—the resiliency of the brain and its remarkable capacity to rebuild itself is truly amazing.

By practicing mindfulness, meditation, and gentle cognitive stimulation, as well as seeking therapy, I gradually restored the pathways disrupted by trauma.

When my grief journey began, I wasn't good at listening to my body. My generation took on the mantra, "No pain, no gain." Resting was a sign of weakness to me. For instance, I often pushed myself to the gym when I felt exhausted instead of relaxing and reflecting on my emotions.

I know I have to feel it to heal it, but what about feeling it in the body?

To be in tune with your emotions, it takes practice listening to your body. It's learning to distinguish our body's emotions and recognize the beliefs that trigger them. We can better understand why we feel certain things when we know our bodies and emotions. Resting and reflecting are equally crucial as pushing and striving to complete tasks. Honoring our emotions and bodies is a sign of strength rather than weakness.

Pay attention to what your body is telling you.

I began taking inventory of my body throughout the day by closing my eyes and asking myself, "How is my body feeling?"

Instead of shaming myself for regularly crying, I extend grace to myself and allow the tears to flow unapologetically. Tears help release stress hormones and, in turn, restore the body to a calmer, more balanced state. They also provide a sense of emotional release, which can be calming and soothing.[61]

Because my physical health is as vital as my emotional health, I rest more, allowing myself to nap or order takeout instead of cooking. Through the haze of decision fatigue, I also explore various avenues of physical healing–the gentle practice of Pilates, walks outside, and riding my Peloton bike all help reestablish strength and flexibility. I mindfully eat nutritious foods to fuel my body to reclaim my physical health. There's transformative power in caring for our bodies, minds, and souls.

**The Transformative Power of Self-Compassion**

In the whirlwind of grief and trauma, I find peace in the most unexpected place– self-compassion. Self-compassion, however, is not self-care. It's not about bubble baths and massages—it's much deeper than that. It's about setting boundaries and learning to say "no" when I need to preserve my energy. It's about seeking support and reaching out to trusted friends and professionals who can lend an empathetic ear and offer guidance. It's about embracing vulnerability, allowing myself to feel the pain, and surrendering to healing.

It feels counterintuitive to prioritize my well-being, especially since I

---

[61] Ad Vingerhoets, *Why Only Humans Weep: Unraveling the Mysteries of Tears* (United Kingdom: OUP Oxford, 2013).

need to ensure my children are thriving. My children's sadness began to be all-consuming, leaving little room for anything else. But as days turned into weeks and weeks into months, neglecting my body only intensified the pain, leaving very little self-preservation to help them.

Embracing our bodies involves extending the same compassion we'd offer to a friend to ourselves. By being gentle with ourselves and recognizing our needs, we enhance our ability to tackle any challenges. This practice empowers us to trust our intuition and make choices rooted in self-love rather than fear and stress.

Self-compassion involves attuning to your body's signals, such as tense shoulders and shallow breaths. Take a moment to relax your muscles, breathe deeply, and inquire about the source of tension instead of ignoring it. Pushing through pain and relying solely on your abilities can result in exhaustion.

Scripture guides us toward surrender, trust, and dependence on God. As the apostle Paul grappled with his weakness, he received a divine response from the Lord, *"My grace is sufficient for you, for my power is made perfect in weakness"* (2 Corinthians 12:9). Our true strength lies not in self-reliance, but in the power of dependence on God.

Acknowledging our body's need for rest isn't a sign of weakness; instead, it reflects God's power. It's an act of wisdom and humility to acknowledge our limitations and turn to God for our true strength. In our exhaustion, God invites us to release the burden of it all on our shoulders and surrender to God's grace and power.

Relying on God allows His power to radiate through us. Surrendering our struggles, weariness, and pain to Him, He empowers us with strength and resilience to navigate the journey of grief and trauma.

Caring for our bodies during these challenging seasons is not a sign of weakness but a testament to our faith and trust in God's provision. It is an act of stewardship, acknowledging that our bodies are temples of the Holy Spirit (1 Corinthians 6:19) and vessels through which His light can shine.

So, dear friend, let us not be deceived by the world's notion of strength that tells us to pull ourselves up by our bootstraps and carry the weight alone. Instead, let us embrace the transformative power of depending on God. Let's rest in His grace, allowing His power to work in and through our weaknesses. For it is in our surrender that His strength shines through, and His healing touch brings wholeness to our weary bodies and souls.

I start with small steps and simple acts of self-care that gradually grow into a powerful healing ritual. During these periods of grief and trauma, I often find peace in the soothing warmth of a bath, letting the water wash away the day's burdens. I revel in the sensation of my feet sinking into the earth; connecting with nature allows me to connect to God. I embrace the therapeutic power of deep breaths, allowing oxygen to infuse the cells with renewed air. Self-care becomes a lifeline that whispers, "You are worthy of love, even in the midst of pain." It becomes a practice of self-compassion, reminding me that healing begins from within.

### Reclaiming Strength: Healing Body and Soul Through Pilates

In the depths of grief and trauma, when my world seems shattered and my spirit fragile, I discovered Pilates.

Right after our world shut down from the COVID virus, a friend opened a Pilates studio, and to my surprise, regularly participating in Pilates benefited not only my body but my mind and soul.

We all know there is overwhelming evidence that exercise improves our mood and physical health. That's why the Psalmist says, *"Though I walk through the valley of death"* (Psalm 23:4). We *move* through our valleys. Movement trains our autonomic nervous system to respond by calming it down. When we feel stuck in our grief or stress rises, let's use motion to open us up to the hope God offers. My mantra became: "I will move my body every day."

As I step into the Pilates studio for the first time, my heart is carrying the weight of sorrow, and my body feels like a vessel of pain. Every movement during class feels daunting, but I am determined to find peace and regain strength amidst the chaos of my grief. Some days, I cry, unable to hold back the sadness, but I think that happens when you move your body—the emotions are released.

Under the gentle guidance of the Pilates instructor, I find the healing connection between breath and movement. Each session becomes a sacred space where I release pent-up emotions. With every controlled stretch and deliberate muscle engagement, I gradually unravel the knots of grief and trauma within my body.

Pilates becomes my sanctuary, where I reconnect with my body and rediscover its resilience. It taught me to listen to my body's whispers, honor its limitations, and trust its healing capacity. With each deliberate movement, I reclaim ownership of my physical being, reclaiming the strength grief and trauma had tried to steal from me.

But it's not just the physical aspect of Pilates bringing healing; it's the mindful nature of the practice that helps cultivate a deep sense of presence and awareness. In those moments of focused concentration, the worries of the past and future anxieties fade. It's teaching me the importance of grounding and living in the present. My breath, sometimes accompanied by tears, helps anchor me to the present moment of healing.

"For real change to take place, the body needs to learn that the danger has passed and to live in the reality of the present."[62]

Pilates becomes more than a physical exercise; it confronts my vulnerabilities, embraces my discomfort, and surrenders to the transformation process. Each session, I discover newfound strength and resilience in my body and spirit. Research proves Pilates and cognitive behavioral therapy reduce anxiety.[63]

The supportive community within the Pilates studio is also instrumental in my healing journey. We share stories, tears, and laughter, creating a web of connection that weaves threads of hope and understanding.

As I learn to take care of my body, I discover I'm also nurturing my soul—a gentle act of self-love that has the power to mend the broken pieces of my being. Pilates taught me the importance of carving out time to nurture my physical and emotional health.

---

[62] van der Kolk, *The Body Keeps the Score*, 21.
[63] Naomi M. Simon et al., "Efficacy of Yoga vs Cognitive Behavioral Therapy vs Stress Education for the Treatment of Generalized Anxiety Disorder," *JAMA Psychiatry* 78, no. 1 (January 1, 2021): 13, https://doi.org/10.1001/jamapsychiatry.2020.2496.

Self-care isn't selfish! It's an act of survival, allowing the body to refuel its depleted energy by finding moments of respite amidst the chaos. It gives us the strength to face the challenges of grief and trauma, armed with a newfound sense of resilience and inner peace. It also allowed us to carry genuine empathy for others.

## DIGGING DEEPER:

1. How did the experience of going through grief and trauma lead to the discovery that self-care is not a luxury but a necessity?

2. How can you prioritize your well-being during this challenging time? How will you lean into the mantra, "We move our bodies daily?" It doesn't have to be Pilates; it can be walking, dancing, biking, weight-lifting, a round of golf, or anything that gets the blood flowing.

3. How can the concept of self-care be a powerful tool for navigating the treacherous road of grief and trauma?

# CHAPTER 15

## THE HEALING
## POWER OF COMMUNITY

*And now God, do it again"–bring rains to our doubt-stricken lives*
*So those who planted their crops in despair will shout hurrahs at the*
*harvest, So those who went off with heavy hearts will come home*
*laughing, with armloads of blessing.*"[64]

While standing in front of our newly constructed home, built on the same foundation, I weep for the layered losses it represents. Just two years ago, I sifted through piles of ash in this very same spot, unable to fix what was lost.

Flames engulfed the twenty years of life my husband and I had built together, and no matter how hard I tried, those ashes wouldn't go back together. Yet, I admire God's handy work, appreciating the beauty of entrusting Him with every aspect of my life, even the difficult ones. In moments when my family faced deep pain and sorrow, and hope felt distant, I realized that we were precisely where God wanted us to be. When the flames engulfed our home, I began my personal rebuilding journey.

---

[64] Psalm 126:4-6 MSG

Further up the driveway, my eye catches the original chimney. It's a miracle that it remains after the fire. The power from the water hoses alone should have knocked it down. In desperation, I asked the Lord to spare it. I thought it would be powerful to tie something from the old house into the new home.

God has a way of using the old to create something even better.

It's not easy. God's hand doesn't instantly sweep away the suffering and dispose of what we lost like unwanted trash. Instead, in the middle of our anguish, He begins a transformation. Grief and loss become the breeding grounds for brokenness transforming into beauty— there's a remaking. A remarkable process unfolds within the fragments of brokenness, similar to the spared chimney attached to our new home.

As much as we want him to, God doesn't erase our pain; rather, He engineers it into the fabric of our existence, weaving it into our lives. This metamorphosis isn't a mere vanishing act; it's an intricate remodeling like turning a dull stone into a precious gem. Rather than discarding the suffering, it becomes an integral part of our story. Through the suffering, God molds us, redefining who we are and infusing it with beauty. Grief becomes a part of us.

Nothing along the path of our journey is ever truly lost. He weaves the grief and trauma into the tapestry of our story. Indeed, some moments may bear the weight of sorrow, yet we must keep our gaze upon Him, trusting in His sovereign plan. Unshakable and unwavering faith in His character remains untouched by the trials we endure.

As I stare at our new home, I envision families gathering in our new kitchen by the warmth of the fireplace, us sharing our story—a testimony of the incredible work God has wrought through these challenging times, all steeped in His boundless love.

"[God] wants to use the harsh conditions of life to shape us–and eventually the whole world–into something extraordinarily beautiful."[65] We long for this transformation, but it can't happen in isolation. Instead, it emerges within community. It's within the sacred company of others,

---

[65] Sittser, *A Grace Disguised*, 19.

as we permit ourselves to embrace our emotions, deepen our communion with God, and harness the profound strength of togetherness, that transformation begins to occur.

My oldest daughter has witnessed the power of togetherness. She's known her whole life that there's a safe place in her mom's arms when life falls apart. It's more than a warm embrace—it's two hearts connecting. What she feels, I feel.

Laughter with laughter. Anguish with anguish. Delight after delight. Tear after tear. Celebration by celebration. Disappointment followed by disappointment. If she can feel it, I can feel it. This special bond transcends physical connection and goes beyond understanding based on our deep emotional relationship. This connection often manifests itself as an unspoken yet tangible understanding between us. It's the ability to feel what touches someone you love.

Time after time, she and I sit together in life's messiness, talking together, thinking together, processing together, holding each other, trying to navigate the grief and trauma together.

Together.

Together is what we need when life falls apart.

As I write this final chapter, my heart is grateful for the immense blessing of my community. Despite all the twists and turns, highs and lows, the power of community shines brightest in those moments of deep sadness.

We see this theme of community resounding in the pages of the Bible. It's a theme that resonates deeply with the fundamental truth that God created us by design for fellowship and connection.

From the beginning of the book of Genesis, we encounter those familiar words: *"It is not good for man to be alone"* (Genesis 1). This foundational declaration sets the stage for the importance of relationships woven throughout the Scriptures. The words *"two are better than one"* in Ecclesiastes remind us of the power of unity and togetherness. According to the Bible, sharing support and uplifting one another magnifies our strength.

The Bible doesn't just speak of community; it teaches us to bear one another's burdens, love our neighbors as ourselves, and practice forgiveness and reconciliation. God intended for us to tackle life's challenges and grow spiritually through our relationships with each other.

There is no better story in the Bible to illustrate the power of comfort through togetherness than Naomi's and Ruth's. Naomi, a widow who had lost her two sons, found herself in deep sorrow and grief. She even changed her name to "Mara," which means "bitter," to reflect her desolation. She had journeyed to Moab with her husband and sons due to famine in their homeland, and there, tragedy had struck, leaving her with nothing but grief.

Ruth, her daughter-in-law, remained steadfast by her side, demonstrating an unwavering commitment to their relationship. Ruth's devotion to Naomi shines with her famous words, *"Where you go, I will go, and where you stay, I will stay. Your people will be my people and your God my God,"* encapsulate the profound connection and support she offered to her grieving mother-in-law (Ruth 1:16).

Through Ruth's presence and loyalty, Naomi found comfort and hope in her darkest hours. Ruth's companionship provided a glimmer of light in Naomi's despair, demonstrating the incredible impact of one person's willingness to stand by another in times of sorrow. Together, they returned to Bethlehem, and in time, their lives began to transform through the kindness and support of their community.

Although the church emphasizes the importance of community, it often fails to embody these ideals in practice. In many instances, the church, with its complex structures and traditions, has inadvertently created an environment where those who are grieving may feel isolated or overlooked. The place meant to be a sanctuary of love and support sometimes becomes a source of added distress for those suffering. Well-meaning clichés or uncomfortable silence are insufficient responses to grief, as grieving is an intensely personal and isolating experience.

There have been instances when the church has struggled to adapt to people's evolving needs and challenges in times of grief. Often, I hear of people leaving the church because there's no space for their pain. "That American tendency toward triumphalism, of optimism rooted in success, money, and privilege, will infect and sap of substance any faith community that has lost its capacity for "holding space" for those in grief."[66]

About ten days after the fire, my two eldest children earnestly pleaded with my husband and me not to attend the Sunday church service this week as a family. When inquiring about their reasons, their voices became vulnerable as they whispered, "We don't want to talk about it with others, and we don't want to feel the awkward silence."

Grief is isolating and often feels like you are drifting in an ocean of sorrow alone. But God calls us to bear one another's burdens. So what do we do when we feel that no one understands? Do we cover our heads in shame, hide under the covers, and pretend all is well?

Tempting.

While we sometimes wish for such an escape, the hurt and wounds will remain. We can't sweep it all under the rug where no one can see in hopes that we will be okay. There's transformation beyond the depths of embracing our emotions.

How do we craft a new life in the wake of loss? How do we submerge ourselves into a community that grapples to fathom our pain?

The answer lies in embracing the fragmented imperfections of our story, for within them lies broken yet breathtaking beauty. It's precisely in the brokenness within a community that the beauty unfolds, for we are all broken people.

We are a community of shattered souls. In our collective brokenness, we find the capacity to sit together to learn the art of loving and supporting one another.

I'm incredibly grateful our family found a safe space in the community around us that showered us with empathy and love. We felt understood and accepted.

---

[66] Rachel Held Evans, *Inspired* (Nashville, TN: Nelson Books, 2018), 110.

I remember the day my dad died. I felt like the world's weight sat on my shoulders. I desperately longed for help, yet it seemed incredibly difficult to ask for it. It wasn't that I was too proud or ashamed to seek help. It's more like my brain fog made it hard to articulate my needs. I had no idea what I needed. This same feeling arose after the fire.

Many people asked, "Let me know what I can do to help." But I didn't know. I may have appeared functional on the outside, but being inundated with calls, texts, and messages from well-meaning friends and family overwhelmed me further. Don't get me wrong, the outpouring of support felt heartwarming. However, I found myself sitting outside, lost in a haze of grief, unable to process it all. I couldn't even begin to fathom what to ask for. I felt stuck, paralyzed by the enormity of my emotions.

But then, amidst the flood of messages. A text came through from a friend; even though she didn't know my dad well, she recognized the depth of my pain. The text read, "Will you be home for a while? I have something to drop off for you."

The support we need doesn't always come from the people closest to us. It comes from unexpected sources, from friends who may not grasp our loss's magnitude but still want to help.

Later that day, the doorbell rang, and my friend stood holding a giant package of paper towels and more paper products in the car. "You always need paper products," she said. We sat for a moment, shedding tears, as I shared stories of my dad.

You don't have to devise grand gestures or quick solutions to fix the pain. You simply show up with open arms, a listening ear, and a willingness to be present. The simple act of my friend showing up reminded me that I didn't have to face grief alone.

In uncertainty, when we're unsure of our needs or how to voice them, there's a possibility that someone may extend a hand and offer comfort through their very presence. However, the pivotal point lies in *accepting* this love and comfort by allowing the protective walls to come down. And as we do, you'll see it's in the sacred exchange that opens ourselves up to vulnerability by inviting others to join us in our healing journey.

## The Ring Theory: A Circle of Compassion in Times of Crisis

We may desire to help others but don't know how or if it's our place to step in to do anything. Understanding how to provide support can profoundly impact the healing process.

In times of crisis, finding the right words or actions to support those directly affected is tricky. It's been over three years of my fight through grief, and I've made it my mission to educate others on how to comfort best those still battling the dark.

Henri Nouwen said, "The word compassion is derived from the Latin words *pati* and *cum*, which together mean 'to suffer with.' Compassion asks us to go where it hurts, enter places of pain, and share in brokenness, fear, confusion, and anguish. Compassion challenges us to cry out with those in misery, mourn with those lonely, and weep with those in tears. Compassion requires us to be weak with the weak, vulnerable with the vulnerable, and powerless with the powerless. Compassion means full immersion in the condition of being human."[67]

Recently, I read about the concept of the Ring Theory —a powerful framework that teaches us how to navigate these challenging moments with empathy and compassion. It helps us to recognize pain and not walk past it.

The Ring Theory, also known as the "kvetching order," was developed by psychologist Susan Silk and writer Barry Goldman. At its core, it revolves around a simple principle: "Comfort in, dump out."

The idea is to draw a circle and then a smaller circle within the larger circle. In the center of this circle, write the name of the person in crisis. Our responsibility as a community lies in the larger circle surrounding the center. Within this ring, we place the names of the people who are next closest to the crisis, such as immediate family or close friends. As we move outward, each subsequent large ring holds the names of the individuals progressively further from the situation. By visualizing this circle, we can better understand the people involved and their proximity to the crisis.

---

[67] Henri Nouwen, *Compassion: A Reflection on the Christian Life* (New York: Image Books, 1983), 4.

Support and comfort flow inward toward the center of the crisis. Those closest to the situation receive the utmost care, understanding, and empathy. My family, for instance, would have been in the innermost ring when our house caught fire as we grappled with the immediate and intense effects of the crisis. In contrast, those in outer rings, who are less directly affected, must be mindful of their interactions and the support they offer. Instead of burdening the center with their emotions or seeking reassurance, they provide a safe and supportive space for those at the core of the crisis. [68]

A few months later, the Ring Theory became helpful when my dear friend began to navigate the treacherous waters of loss. Watching her struggle brought on a deep sense of helplessness. I yearned to be there for her, yet I didn't know where to start.

Helping someone can start with a simple yet profound question: "Where am I in the circle, and how can I help them feel less alone in their grief?"

It often begins with listening.

She pours out her anguish and sorrow, and I listen without judgment or interruption. In that sacred space, comfort flows freely, and her emotions find refuge. Over the next few days, we exchange frequent text messages; I seek to remind her relentlessly that she is not alone.

The late-night phone conversations, holding her hand through tear-soaked conversations, and accompanying her to the memorial service helped her feel less alone in her grief.

My dear friend, this is the profound impact of the Ring Theory in my life!

In the past few years, I've shared the concept of the Ring Theory with our mutual friends and acquaintances, encouraging them to be mindful of their interactions with grieving friends and family. It's not about saying the right words but being there for each other. Together, we form a circle of compassion, a safety net, around others grieving–this is empathy.

---

[68] Elana Premack Sandler, "Ring Theory Helps Us Bring Comfort In," *Psychology Today*, 2017, https://www.psychologytoday.com/us/blog/promoting-hope-preventing-suicide/201705/ring-theory-helps-us-bring-comfort-in.

Sometimes, actions speak louder than words. The simplest acts of kindness mean far more than doing nothing. Running errands, cooking meals, and shouldering some of her daily burdens were significant gestures conveying our deep understanding of her pain and our unwavering commitment to stand by her side.

In those shared moments, there are no comparisons, no recounting of other losses, no attempts to relate by drawing parallels with someone else's grief. Instead, it's about focusing on the unique journey of grief or trauma, giving each other the space to express emotions without feeling overshadowed.

Respecting boundaries is a guiding principle when supporting someone in grief and trauma. I remember some days when I'd seek solitude and quiet reflection, while others, I'd welcome company. Recognizing and respecting these shifts demonstrates an understanding of what the other person needs and readiness to support them however they need, without getting frustrated.

I would share my frustrations and anger, finding comfort in having someone who listened without judgment. Releasing emotions during the healing process is crucial, and having someone who listens without judgment provides a safe space to express feelings openly.

We often hold back from reaching out to others, assuming someone else is handling it. However, building a supportive community where everyone feels included requires us to let go of hesitations and take proactive steps. It's a joint effort—a shared commitment.

Together, we can leave an enduring mark on those navigating the stormy seas of challenging times.

It's our mission.

It's clear in 1 Peter: *"Summing up: Be agreeable, be sympathetic, be loving, be compassionate, be humble. That goes for all of you, no exception. No retaliation. No sharp-tongued sarcasm. Instead, bless—that's your job, to bless. You'll be a blessing and also get a blessing."* [69]

A profound revelation occurs when we walk together through anguish and sorrow: We're not alone. Those tears that fell, the weight of

---

[69] 1 Peter 3:8 MSG

grief that pressed upon our hearts, the anxious thoughts that consumed us, the physical ailments that weakened our bodies, and the inability to pull ourselves up by our bootstraps—none of these were indicative of our lack of faith or a mark of weakness. It's all a normal part of grief.

Because we now know we're not alone.

A few months ago, with trembling hands and a deep yearning to embody our grief, my husband and I shared our story for the first time at a retreat center. In an effort to let others know they aren't alone in their pain, we held nothing back, revealing every aspect of our journey—losing my dad, my mom's sudden battle with cancer, the devastating house fire that robbed us of everything, a challenging month-long hospital stay with a son born with half a heart, and the emotional journey of guiding five kids through grief and anxiety, one of whom struggled with addiction.

Through our tears, healing unfolded. Sharing our broken yet beautiful story gave words not only to our grief and pain but also to those who listened. Opening ourselves up to the depth of our emotions created a connection, allowing our brokenness to resonate with the brokenness of others.

I pray my story weaves into yours as well. I pray you know I'm standing with you, reaching for your hand. Grab hold. Return from the place of loneliness and the darkest place of your soul, and catch your breath, knowing you're not alone.

Having come out on the other side, I now know I did not suffer because of God's wrath or His desire for me to learn some profound truth. Instead, each moment of pain provided an invitation in which I could experience His love more deeply. Although I don't understand all the reasons, His constant presence and love through it was never in question.

My family engaged in fierce battles and heated arguments. There were mornings when I woke up uncertain about my son's well-being and many nights when I cried myself to sleep, overwhelmed by the uncertainty of how everything would unfold. In those moments that threatened to consume me, I found peace in God's unwavering, ever-present, and profound love.

But God, here we are, gathering around our long farm table in front of the saved chimney for my birthday dinner. Seeing my vision become a reality is almost unbearable. Looking around the table nearly takes my breath away. I'm overwhelmed by God's goodness. Oh, how I yearn for it all to have never unfolded. I wish the path had been smoother, the burdens less weighty.

I wish my son had never grappled with addiction, yet I am profoundly grateful he is flourishing in his recovery. Never in a million years did I envision my children losing everything, but here they are with a profound resilience in the wake of their pain and anxiety.

While there are days when I deeply miss my father, I am equally thankful for the precious years we shared. I long for the magic recipe that could banish the pain and bring an end to these relentless trials. I wish I possessed a red bow to neatly wrap around it all, assuring you life is nothing but a collection of fairy-tale endings, but it's not.

Although life takes unexpected turns, God's hand remains evident.

Life becomes sweeter in complexity, and our appreciation for it deepens as we allow ourselves the freedom to feel. Because of this, I know with my entire being that God is alive and present, and there is no doubt that He will never leave or forsake us. No matter how bruised and wounded we become, He is always there waiting with open arms to comfort us. His presence is our strength to make it through another day.

I leave you with these words: *"If your heart is broken, you'll find God right there; if you're kicked in the gut, he'll help you catch your breath"* (Psalm 24:18).

## DIGGING DEEPER:

1. Take inventory of your life and journal how you've seen God's hand throughout your journey of suffering.

2. Thank people who have been there for you, telling them how their compassion has impacted your journey.

# THANKS

I want to thank…..

The Lord who beckons the hurting, wounded ones, wooing us with intimate grace, and binds our wounds with His love. He tenderly met me, revealing Himself in new ways along this journey and showing me that He can do more than I ask or imagine immeasurably.

It would be impossible for me to reach my goals without the support of my husband, Mike. You filled in the gaps, so I had the time to write this book. Thank you for loving me well and anticipating my needs throughout this journey. I can never thank you enough.

My fellow members of the *Beaten But Not Forgotten Club*, Rachel and Angel, for holding space for all my grief and trauma and allowing me to show up raw and vulnerable. I could not have made it without both of you. Thank you for reading and correcting my manuscript.

My sister, Michele who prayed and loved relentlessly, making me feel less alone in the world.

My sister-in-love, Julie, for giving me the space to laugh and cry through the hard. Unfortunately, we share a similar heartache, but I am thankful for growing and learning through it together.

Beautiful souls, you each opened the door to more of God. Thank you for pushing me to make this dream a reality.

To my friend, Faith, who'd travel the world with me if I asked and who's never judged me even at my worst.

My mom—for being my biggest fan and helping pick up the slack while I wrote daily. Your constant prayers and support have been the grace needed to finish well.

My dad–for ushering in this season and teaching me the power of forgiveness. I miss you each and every day. I know you would be proud of me.

Our Columbus and church family who showed up for us in unexpected ways, making us feel loved and cared for.

To any woman, I've had the privilege to lead through Bible studies who's shared a bit of their unspoken brokenness with me.

To my readers who have traveled with me through this writing journey, these pages are for you and because of you.

The gifted authors at HopeBooks, thank you for all your support and encouragement along the way; it indeed has been a privilege and a joy to run this race with all of you. I believe I've made some lifelong friends.

To Brian Dixon and the HopeBooks team for making a dream a reality. There aren't enough words to express my gratitude.

www.ingramcontent.com/pod-product-compliance
Lightning Source LLC
Chambersburg PA
CBHW020234130626
46549CB00005B/1881